D0184519

WITHDRAWN FROM
NEWCASTLE

Newcastle
City Council

Newcastle Libraries and Information Service

O1 HO  **0191 277 4100**

Due for return	Due for return	Due for return
1.5 JUN 2010		
1 3 JUL 2010		

Please return this item to any of Newcastle's Libraries by the last
date shown above. If not requested by another customer the
loan can be renewed, you can do this by phone, post or in person.
Charges may be made for late returns.

HISTORY
OF THE
BRITISH TROLLEYBUS

Other Bus histories

Colin Morris—History of the Hants & Dorset Motor Services
John Hibbs—The History of British Bus Services
R. C. Anderson and G. Frankis—History of Royal Blue Express Services

HISTORY
OF THE
BRITISH TROLLEYBUS

NICHOLAS OWEN

DAVID & CHARLES
NEWTON ABBOT LONDON
NORTH POMFRET (VT) VANCOUVER

0 7153 6370 0

© NICHOLAS OWEN 1974

All rights reserved. No part of this publication may be reproduced, stored in a retrieval system, or transmitted, in any form or by any means, electronic, mechanical, photocopying, recording or otherwise, without the prior permission of David & Charles (Holdings) Limited

NEWCASTLE UPON TYNE
CITY LIBRARIES

Class No.	Acc. No. CS
388·46	811810 A
Checked	Issued
BA	6/9/74

GALAXY 2000

Set in 10 on 12 pt .Monotype Bembo and printed in Great Britain by John Sherratt & Son Ltd. at the St Ann's Press, Park Road, Altrincham for David & Charles (Holdings) Limited, South Devon House, Newton Abbot, Devon

Published in the United States of America by David & Charles Inc., North Pomfret, Vermont 05053

Published in Canada by Douglas David & Charles Limited, 3645 McKechnie Drive, West Vancouver, B.C.

For
Philippa
and
Rebecca

CONTENTS

LIST OF ILLUSTRATIONS

MAPS

DIAGRAMS, LINE DRAWINGS AND GRAPHS

ACKNOWLEDGEMENTS

Thanks go to the following for permission to reproduce the plates on the following pages: R. N. Ashton, 144 (*bottom*); Ian Ballam, 125 (*bottom*), 143 (*top*); Belfast Corporation Transport, 89 (*bottom*), 107 (*top*); D. G. Bowen, 126 (*top*); Bradford City Transport, 26 (*top*), 28 (*top*), 125 (*left*); A. S. Crosley, 25 (*bottom*); Glasgow Corporation Transport, 108 (*bottom*); the Librarian, Hove Public Library, 27; Huddersfield Examiner, 126 (*bottom*); Fred Ivy, frontispiece; Leeds City Transport, 26 (*bottom*), 28 (*bottom*), 144 (*top*); London Transport, 25 (*top*), 71, 72 (*bottom*), 89 (*top*); Maidstone District Motor Services, 54 (*bottom*); Roy Marshall, 107 (*bottom*); Metro-Cammell Weymann, 72 (*top*); Museum of English Rural Life, University of Reading, 54 (*top*), 90 (*top*); Clough Smith and A. G. Ratcliffe, 53, 90 (*bottom*); Iain Whitlam, 108 (*top*), 143 (*bottom*).

INTRODUCTION

IT was H. E. Bates in the Preface to his delightful book *My Uncle Silas* who wrote: 'I have always thought it a fatal policy for an author to set out to explain his own work . . .' It is a very good principle, but like him, I think a few brief lines are required on the composition of *History of the British Trolleybus*. The important point is that I have tried to cover the subject as a student of transport affairs, rather than as a trolleybus enthusiast. This accounts for the comparative lack of lists, either of vehicles or routes, or whatever. I have sought the essential pattern of trolleybus development in this country as a whole. The written account is, I hope, comprehensive, but it should be said that the choice of pictures and the maps and diagrams drawn have largely been the product of personal choice. An attempt to depict every vehicle type would fill the book with pictures; a determination to reproduce every route would result in a mere map collection.

The only other point is my choice of the word 'trolleybus' throughout. The permutations of this apparently simple term are numerous, the most common being trolley bus or trollybus. My selection was determined by the word used in London, my own nearest and dearest system; sufficient justification, I hope.

An extensive list of written sources starts on page 179, but a large amount of the information gathered for the book came from individuals and organisations. I am bound to leave out someone who has helped in an important way, to whom I offer automatic apologies. The following list is alphabetical for fairness.

All corporations and transport bodies approached were most co-operative. Help was given by: Bournemouth Corporation and David Chalk; Bradford Corporation and the City Transport department; Derby Corporation and T. W. W. Knowles; Doncaster Corporation; the Museum and Art Galleries Department of Dundee Corporation; the Borough of Epsom and Ewell; Glasgow Corporation; Hull Transport Department; Leeds City Transport and John Blakeborough; London Transport; Maidstone & District and S. C. Wicks; the City Records Office in Portsmouth; Stroud Urban District Council; and Tyneside Passenger Transport Executive, particularly J. M. Smith.

Several companies gave up valuable time to get the story straight: Brecknell, Willis & Co at Chard and M. E. Hopkins; British Leyland Motor Corporation; GEC Traction and N. Gardener; Hawker Siddeley; and Ransomes, Sims & Jefferies.

Other help came from: the Chartered Institute of Transport; the Department of the Environment; Institution of Electrical Engineers; Museum of English Rural Life, University of Reading; Patent Office National Reference Libraries; and the Science Museum Library.

Special thanks are due to all the individuals who either gave or made available information: D. G. Bowen of Cardiff; A. J. Braddock, secretary of the National Trolleybus Association; R. Edgley Cox, former manager at Walsall; Edward Croot, of BBC Leeds who helped trace the 1911 routes; A. S. Crosley, former RET draughtsman who kindly let me consult documents assembled for his interesting 1961 paper on trolleybus development as well as recalling the pre World War I days; Peter Greenhow, who really set me on the trail in the first place; Fred Ivy, involved with the British Trolleybus Society and the London Trolleybus Preservation Society; Charles E. Lee, the renowned transport historian; Roy Makewell, another London Trolleybus Preservation Society stalwart; Martin Nimmo, who gave invaluable aid of all sorts; A. G. Ratcliffe, many years in charge of Clough Smith's overhead installation, to whom I offer particular thanks for allowing access to documents and pictures; Nick Skinner, who willingly assisted with preparing photographs; and John Whitehead, of the British Trolleybus Society, to whom I am grateful particularly for filling in gaps in the stories of Guy, Garrett, Sunbeam and Railless among the manufacturers.

In a place deservedly apart, I would like to thank four Bradford residents who have let me share their love for that fine and longest-running network: Harold Brearley, an acknowledged authority on trolleybuses everywhere; Arthur Green, who following a chance meeting, got together impressions of driving in the early days; Stanley King, local councillor and trolleybus supporter, who deserves a medal for checking the manuscript; and Edgar Oughtibridge, who worked on the original vehicles, and was guest of honour on the last one.

Specific permission to quote various material is acknowledged with thanks. Allen West of Brighton permitted reproductions of the driving instructions on page 60; Brecknell, Willis & Co the trolley head drawing on page 55; the British Electrical and Allied Manufacturers Association, the poem on page 59 adapted from 'The Walrus and the Carpenter'; and the list of preserved vehicles on page 173 is based on one which appeared in British Trolley Bus Scene, published by Turntable Enterprises.

As a working journalist I have been appreciative of the help extended by newspapers mentioned among the sources; I would specially thank the *Daily Telegraph* for using the feature which 'gave birth' to the project.

Of all the many expressions of 'thank you' the largest and most heartfelt goes to my wife, who not only endured the tribulations of research, but also typed the manuscript so willingly and well.

Having named the names who helped, in large measure or small, I must point out that all errors of fact and interpretation which may become apparent are entirely my responsibility.

Redhill, Surrey NICHOLAS OWEN

CHAPTER ONE

THE PIONEERS

THE meeting of Dundee's tramways committee on 10 July 1908, brought together a group of councillors who had been responsible for building up an efficient and progressive electric tram system inaugurated almost exactly eight years earlier. That particular day they were ready to listen, intrigued, to the report of a visit to the Continent of Europe by the system's manager, Peter Fisher, his electrical engineer, and two members of the committee. They had left Scotland for Germany on 12 June. The phlegmatic group would probably have given scant thought to the historic nature of their deputation, which was the first from Britain to investigate the latest development in public transport—the trackless car. 'This new system,' explained the Dundee report, 'might be described as a motor car or motor bus obtaining its energy from an overhead wire instead of carrying a prime mover on each individual vehicle. The power is obtained from overhead wires just as is the case an ordinary electric tramway, with this difference, that two wires are required overhead instead of one, the one wire being the positive and the other the negative side of the electric circuit.'

Mr Fisher, committee convenor Alexander Speed, councillor G. A. Johnston, and H. Richardson, the engineer, had first seen trackless at Monheim, near Dusseldorf. Cars ran for 2½ miles between the town and the local railway station. When the deputation arrived, rails were being laid, the trackless vehicles having generated enough traffic to justify such capital expenditure. Similar development was planned for Dundee's Clepington Road route. At the station served by the Monheim system, overhead wires carried on into the railway yard and goods were transported in a trailer towed by the car. Next, the Dundee sub-committee visited Ahrweiler, where a trackless network had been opened in May 1906. Twenty passengers could be carried in each vehicle, the same number in a coupled trailer.

Finally, the Dundee representatives went to Mulhausen 'where the very

17

latest example of this system of traction can be seen'. Trackless cars—the expression which was to be used in Britain came from the German 'Gleislose Spurwagen' or trackless tram—were put on to serve the town zoo, which was at the top of a steep hill. Experimental running had taken place between 4 and 17 May that year 'with satisfactory results'. Unfortunately, while state officials from Strasbourg were inspecting the system, a car got out of control on the hill. 'But for the excellent steering arrangements on the car, and the coolness of the driver, serious consequences might have resulted. Carriages and other obstructions were on the street, a dangerous curve with a bridge was at the bottom of the hill, and while the driver was unable to retard the progress of the car he was able to steer it clear of all danger.'

Better brakes were fitted to the cars, but, in the meantime, a row developed between the state authorities and the municipality over whether the trackless represented a railway, with all the necessary statutory requirements. It was an argument which soon cropped up in Britain. Mulhausen's cars were kept out of service until the dispute was settled, and the Dundee party had to inspect the cars at the shed.

Nevertheless, the Scotsmen were impressed enough to conclude that 'The trackless trolley system of traction is undoubtedly practicable and well suited for routes where the traffic would not warrant the construction of an ordinary tramway, and the sub-committee are satisfied that there is more likelihood of success with this system than any other'. To support their case, they showed lantern slides of the German cars.

Dundee was not the first authority to consider trackless, and even though its representatives had troubled to get first-hand impressions, the tramways committee voted to suspend judgement on trackless operation until other British undertakings adopted it and allowed studies closer to home. Yet the interest shown typified the thinking of go-ahead operators who had kept informed of the work being carried out in Germany, France, Italy and Austria. The United States too was developing such vehicles, but the sheer difficulty of communication, exemplified by newspaper reports which seemed to treat the whole of America like a vast Wild West, precluded much influence from across the Atlantic.

Credit for the invention of the trackless car goes undoubtedly to Werner von Siemens, the German electrical engineer who, with Johann Halske, founded the electrical firm which bears his name. In 1881, when he was 45, Siemens designed current collection gear fitted to an open, four-wheel carriage which could seat about five people in comfort. A flexible cable was attached to a 5 ft high pole positioned in the middle of the vehicle. Two 2.2 kW motors were fitted under the driver's seat. According to a Berlin electrical magazine in the late 1940s, permission to run Siemens' 'Elektromote' in the city was obtained on 6 October 1881. A line 540 metres long was erected in Halensee and the first demonstration was held the following 29 April. The large, horse-buggy type of rear wheels were driven by chain reduction gear. It is recorded that the vehicle was modified in June, and appears to have run for about three months.

Little more was done in Europe until the turn of the century, but in the meantime various American electrical engineers kept busy. A photograph exists of a vehicle similar to Siemens' Elektromote reputedly taken in 1885 in Nevada, and a five-wheel vehicle, with one pivoted in front for steering, was depicted in 1889. American development was chronicled in the *Financial Times* for 7 September 1897, which alongside an article discussing the Chinese slave trade, reported the running of overhead trolley vehicles 'on an ordinary road, without going to the expense of laying steel rails'. Such experiments were being carried out in New England, although the paper thought a 'wonderful change' would have to come over American roads before such traction could be widely adopted. Three days before, a most intriguing reference had appeared in the *Autocar* to an 'electric omnibus supplied with current from an overhead wire'. The surprising element is that trials were apparently being made on a ¾ mile run in Greenwich, south east London, but all records of such an event have disappeared.

Basic trackless development took an important step forward in 1899 when Siemens demonstrated a 7½ hp motor capable of 28 kmh on a level road. Into the picture soon afterwards came Max Schiemann, connected with the Siemens and Halske business in Berlin, who perfected the 'under running' collector system whereby the stiffened booms ran underneath two parallel wires. Using this system, the first public trackless route was opened at Bielethal, near Königstein, on 10 July 1901. Soon afterwards, similarly-equipped vehicles began running near Lyons in France. By 1910, seven Schiemann systems were operating in Germany plus one in Norway.

One of these was the Mulhausen line, which was visited by the Dundee party. The cars used had one motor to drive each rear wheel, and this development led to the setting up on 7 July 1908, of Railless Electric Traction, the company which was to bring the first trolleybuses to Britain. Before detailing the group's progress, it is interesting that some municipalities had already sketched out proposals with the continental systems in mind. The earliest definite plan appears to have been in Stroud, Gloucestershire, which in 1902-3 proposed an electric trolley service to five towns in the Stroud valley. The network was to be financed by local businessmen, led by George Holloway,

founder of the friendly societies movement. The project was killed however
when the Great Western Railway speeded up plans to put on steam railcars for
local services. About the same period, Rochester, Chatham, Gravesend and
Maidstone Tramways envisaged cars 'on the overhead trolley system and not
running on fixed rails,' but its 1903 Bill was abandoned. In 1908 itself, trackless
lines were envisaged between Edinburgh and Dalkeith, and at Malvern,
Middlesbrough, Oldham, and Salford.

The architect of the Railless Electric Traction concern, holding the British
licence for Schiemann, was a Bristol man, Edward May Munro. In his home
town, he had helped found the overhead firm of Brecknell, Munro and Rogers,
and had worked on the wiring for St Petersburg's electric trams in 1904 and
1905. A short, thick-set man in his mid fifties, who suffered somewhat from
asthma, Mr Munro became chief engineer of Railless, which had been formed
with a capital of £4,750 in £1 shares. The investors included notables of the
time like Sir Alexander Gibbons, Sir Salter Pyne, Sir James d'Houghton, and a
certain J. Armfield, whose father ran a businessman's hotel opposite Railless's
first Moorgate Street office in the City of London. The company secretary
was H. H. Bathurst, a nephew of Lord Bathurst. The first chairman was Lord
Headley, who was known as the Mohammedan peer for his exploits out East.
A Cornish financier, Julian Polglace, was the first managing director, succeeded
in 1913 by Bertram Fox of the famous civil engineering family. It looks as
though the shareholders were to get little return for their money.

At any rate, Railless's chance to prove what it could offer came in September
1909, when it set up a length of overhead at the Hendon depot of Metropolitan
Electric Tramways and proceeded to demonstrate with a single-deck car. A
15-page brochure was prepared which declared the vehicle incorporated the
best of continental practice with 'many new features'. Mr Munro stressed that
the overhead equipment of any planned trackless system should be up to
tramway standard as routes 'may themselves afterwards be converted to
tramway lines when the traffic was sufficiently developed to justify the extra
cost of rails'. This is firm evidence that what was to become the trolleybus was
never intended as tram replacement material. Straightforward twin wire was
erected at first, but a triple-wire system was installed later, presumably because
of insulation problems. A pair of hooters were fitted inside the vehicle, one to
warn of current leakage and the other reversal of polarity, in which case a
switch had to be thrown.

Among the list of advantages was that the car was 'able to accommodate
itself to the exigencies of the traffic, and pass obstructions with the same facility
as any other type of mechanically-propelled road vehicle'. The brochure

added: 'Although installations of this character are as yet confined to the continent, a consideration of the special features and advantages of Railless Traction demonstrates that the conditions most favourable for the system are realized to a peculiar degree in this country.'

The vehicle had been built to the specification of MET, with the chassis probably constructed at Hammersmith by James and Browne. The 22-seat body was provided by Milnes, Voss of Birkenhead, and power came from two 25 hp BTH motors. The car was painted in MET livery, numbered 1, and carried boards advertising a ficticious route from The Burroughs Hendon to Golders Green Station. Running on a short U-shaped line, which included a 1 in 9 gradient, started on 25 September. A speed of 15 mph was sometimes reached, and visitors were reported impressed.

Keeping a strict chronological check on British trackless progress around this period is difficult: there were varying influences on potential operators manifest at different times. Dundee's trail-blazing deputation predated by 15 months the Railless demonstrations at Hendon, yet the Railless company had been formed before the Dundee men reported back to their transport committee. The next deputation to venture overseas was sent from Sheffield in January 1909, and took three days to reach Vienna, where trackless cars operated on a different sort of collection system, Mercedes-Stoll. Current was taken through a four-wheel carriage running on top of two closely-placed wires, the gear being attached to the vehicle with a flexible cable. The Vienna cars had two 20 hp motors, with seats for 12 and standing room for the same number. Each vehicle would cost about £800 and running costs were put at 4½d per mile. The Sheffield deputation travelled on to Mulhausen, where, like the Dundee people, they saw four cars working with the Schiemann system. Finally they inspected the first Filovia-equipped system, perfected in Italy by Dr A. M. Zani, and used on a route between Pescara and Castellamare, opened in 1904. Zani's equipment was a four-wheel carriage running underneath twin wires. Sheffield's representatives urged adoption of the Mercedes (or Cedes)-Stoll principle, but the proposal was deferred.

A similar itinerary was followed by a delegation from Leeds, which set off on a 35-hour rail journey to Vienna on 6 April 1909. The members were met by the managing director of the Vienna layout, and Herr Stoll, inventor of the collection system. The Leeds deputation was allowed the use of Vienna council's own ornate car to tour the system. Also inspected was a six-mile trackless route at Wiedling, 15 miles along the Danube from the Austrian capital; then it was on to Milan and Dr Zani. Finally the three Leeds councillors and general manager J. B. Hamilton saw the Mulhausen company-operated network.

On 27 November that year, a big deputation left Bradford for the continent. This was a more 'high-powered' affair, the intention being not only to study trackless operations, but also make a review of general transport practice. Included were Ald. Enoch Priestley, chairman of the tramways committee, Ald Wesley Knight, three councillors, general manager Christopher John Spencer, and engineer W. H. S. Dawson. They first visited Berlin, with its 2,700 tramcars, before moving on to Vienna and its trackless vehicles. They were received by Herr Spangler, the general manager, who must have been getting used to British faces! Each car was 'practically without noise' and 'almost as free in its use of the road as a self-propelled type of vehicle,' stated the deputation's report. Running costs tallied with figures given to the Leeds party, and Bradford's deputation noted that overhead installation worked out between £700 and £800 a mile. However, wooden poles and other cheap short cuts were used: it was estimated that the cost in England would be between £1,200 and £1,500. A small system at Klosterneuberg, about 20 miles from Vienna, was also studied. Cedes equipment was in use, and when cars from opposite directions met, collection cables had to be unplugged and exchanged.

The Bradford deputation carried on to Munich. There were no trackless cars there, but two interesting points were noted, one with approval, the other not: route numbers were in use (they had in fact been introduced to London in 1906) ... and women changed the points! From Munich they travelled to meet Dr Zani in Milan. He showed them the remarkable Filovia line which climbed from Argegno on Lake Como to St Fedele, 656 ft up on a mountain ridge. For 5½ miles there was an average gradient of 1 in 16½, the worst being 1 in 7. There were several hairpin bends, at which the trolley cars had to reverse to get round, despite their short, 9 ft wheelbases. The cars were equipped with two 12 hp series-parallel motors. It was a fine example of what trackless cars could do, and there had been no serious interruptions since the opening. The Lake Como line was 'no speculative experiment but is a good engineering proposition and capable of considerable utilisation,' the Bradford team observed. When it reached Mulhausen, the deputation thought the Schiemann system there out of date and with no special features. After taking in the trams of Cologne and Brussels, the Bradford worthies arrived home and recommended either the Cedes or Filovia systems. A year later trackless operation would start—with Schiemann equipment!

Councillors and officials felt that all had gone well, friendly receptions being encountered everywhere, evidence of an 'excellent spirit' among tramway operators. 'The deputation are unanimously of the opinion that the wisdom of the council has been more than justified in sending out a deputation to the

Continent' the report commented. A good time it seems was had by all.

The result was the promotion in Parliament of Bills to run trackless vehicles in Leeds and Bradford and in mid-1910 developments were exciting the 'keenest interest' among transport undertakings in the words of the *Tramway and Railway World*. Natural rivalry has long existed between the two communities but at some stage they both picked Mr Munro's Railless group (called RET Construction after March 1911) to carry out the installation work and supply of cars. And probably to ease negotiations with the company, it was decided to open on the same day, 20 June 1911. Originally Bradford looked all set to win the 'race'. The corporation had been informed that a route would open at the end of March equipped with two Filovia cars ordered from Dr Zani. Regular services were due to start in mid-April but the plan was ruined when delivery of the vehicles was delayed. In the event two rear-entrance RET cars numbered 240 and 241 were bought. Leeds took four front entrance cars nos 501-4. The chassis were by Alldays and Onions of Birmingham and the bodies by Hurst Nelson a Motherwell firm. The overall length was 20 ft 3 in; wheelbases 13 ft; seating was for 28; the 525-volt power supply drove two 20 hp Siemens motors; the hand controller had nine forward and six reverse notches with no provision for rheostatic braking; and the cost was £700 per car. Overhead installation costs were expected to be £1,300 a mile for the Leeds route (covering 4 miles from Thirsk Row adjoining City Square to Farnley Moor Top) and £1,250 at Bradford (a 1¼ mile route being equipped from Laisterdyke to Dudley Hill).

About six trial runs were made on the Bradford stretch prior to opening, and probably a similar number were arranged in Leeds. The latter deserves the distinction of the 'first', even though both trackless operations began officially at noon on the 20th, which was a Tuesday. Attentions were focussed on the coronation of George V on the Thursday; Leeds put its cars straight into service to bring celebrating crowds into the city. Bradford had to delay regular operation until after the coronation while the formal report of the Board of Trade inspecting officer, Major J. W. Pringle, was prepared. He had seen the layout on the 19th.

At the wheel of the first Leeds car, no 503, as it left Thirsk Row was the Lord Mayor, Ald. William Middlebrook, who was, incidentally, an enthusiastic motorist. The local Press reported that the fare was 3d and the round trip took three-quarters of an hour. One-man running had been planned, but the number of passengers forced the use of conductors.

The opening ceremony was followed by a luncheon at the Town Hall, attended by 200 guests, who included a most important contingent—representatives from Bradford who had just inaugurated their own trackless system. At Bradford's Laisterdyke terminus, a rostrum had been erected for the speech-making. The Lord Mayor, Ald. Jacob Moser, probably had other more pressing problems on his mind, for the city was in the grip of a serious woolcombers' strike, and he was acting as mediator. The dispute in fact delayed his departure for the coronation. Most of the appropriate words came from Ald. Priestley, chairman of the tramways committee, who said that a tram line had been considered to Dudley Hill, but heavy capital costs ruled it out. Leeds too had wanted trams along the Whitehall Road to Farnley as far back as 1901, but had encountered opposition to crossing the city boundary from adjoining rural district councils. In his speech, Ald. Priestley recalled the continental deputation which had investigated the worth of trackless schemes. Then the Lord Mayor waved the first car, with councillors aboard, on its way. He did not sample the new mode of transport himself, instead mounting the tramcar which set off via Stanningley and its unique gauge-changing point to Leeds, and the luncheon. It was by all accounts a jolly occasion, and gave rise to at least one misapprehension. Bradford's general manager, Mr Spencer, apologised jokingly that his watch had been half-an-hour fast and so his trackless car had accidentally been the country's first. Mr Hamilton, his Leeds' counterpart, quipped back: 'Mine was half a day fast!' The exchange gave birth to the story believed by many early crews in Leeds that they had really got in ahead.

The Bradford *Daily Telegraph*, putting the trackless event on its back page on a day dominated by coronation news, praised the 'neat' cars and reported that the half-hour frequency of the service would probably be increased to 20 minutes. The *Weekly Telegraph* published the following weekend headed its article 'Bradford Trolley 'Buses', going on to talk of complaints about the 1d fare. Passengers were suggesting that the route should be divided into two ½d stages. In the succeeding months, trackless cars did not enjoy great popularity. Dewirements were frequent, and because of the poor state of the roads, vibration was intense. The public which had lined the route out of curiosity on the first day began calling the vehicles 'reckless' and the 'penny joss' because of the 'jossing' up and down. Drivers chewed peanuts to keep their mouths moist as dust swirled into their faces. Trackless cabs were tiny, so only the smallest tram drivers were picked for the new cars. No 240 worked alone for a few weeks until 241 arrived as a stand-in.

Financially, Bradford's trackless cars looked promising. The annual figures to 31 March 1912, showed the new vehicles had travelled 28,115 miles and receipts totalled £848, averaging 7.23d per car mile. The trackless deficit was £48. The following year, they ran 41,658 miles, and receipts had risen to

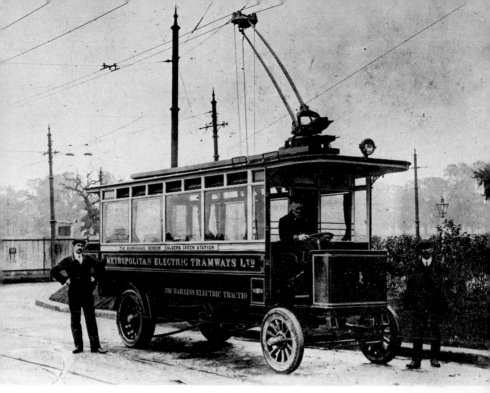

Page 25. (*above*) Britain's first trolleybus in 1909.
(*below*) Many transport managers pocketed these
visiting cards before 1914

E. M. Munro, M.I.Mech.E. M.I.E.E.

Messrs Brecknell, Munro & Rogers, Ltd.

Electrical & Mechanical Engineers.

Thrissell Street Works,
Lawrence Hill, Bristol.

THE "R.E.T." SYSTEM.
("THE TROLLEY BUS.")

A. S. CROSLEY.

THE R.E.T. CONSTRUCTION CO., LTD.,
56, MOORGATE STREET, E.C.

Page 26. The pioneers. (*above*) Bradford's first car, and (*below*) Leeds' first at Farnley terminus

Page 27. (*above*) Brighton tried the first double-decker in 1913, and next-door Hove later experimented with a Cedes-Stoll vehicle (*below*)

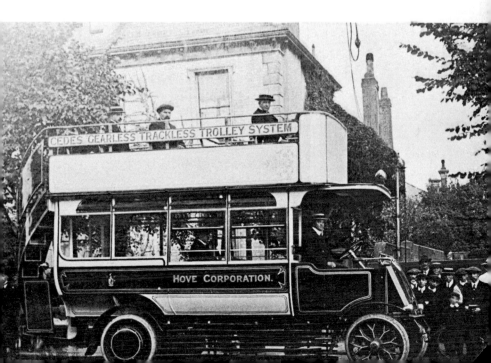

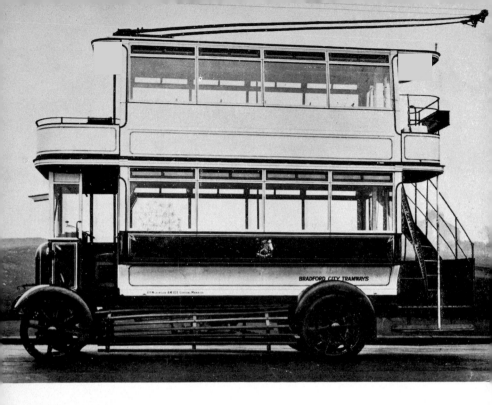

Page 28. (*above*) The first enclosed double-decker: Bradford 521, built 1920. Note hand controller. (*below*) Leeds double-deckers with the first, 510, on right

£1,234. But the mile average had slipped to 7.1d. Mr Spencer put the 1912-13 loss at just over £380, but pointed out to the tramways committee that the cars' value in 'feeding' custom to the busy tram lines was not possible to quantify. He thought the initial route too short to be economically useful. A second generation of cars was on its way; despite passengers' irritations, he defended 240 and 241. 'They have been very reliable for a new system and our troubles in connection therewith have been of a very minor character.'

Mr Spencer stands out, with Mr Munro, as one of the trolleybus pioneers, a man of exceptional character who had been appointed general manager in 1898 when he was only 22. His father had been manager of Halifax Tramways, and he had an apprenticeship with Blackpool Tramways. He had urged adoption of railless from about 18 months before the Bradford opening. During the 1914-18 war, Mr Spencer organised shipyard labour for the Admiralty and afterwards became manager of London United Tramways, destined to be the first undertaking in the capital to use trolleybuses. Before the Bradford inauguration he had spent 36 days obtaining information from other managers, and the cost of this was reported to the tramways committee as £55. Expert witnesses' fees at the Parliamentary hearing which preceded the granting of trackless powers amounted to £101; and that deputation to the continent cost the city £261. In an early report to his committee after the 1911 start, Mr Spencer, expressing his satisfaction at the new operation, said the contractors had to make occasional visits to attend to the equipment. So it was an exceptionally busy time for Mr Munro, who after a day's work in London would forsake his Chelsea home and catch the 6 pm train north from St Pancras. In the other direction, Mr Hamilton of Leeds would often go to London to see RET about problems; Mr Spencer is recalled as a rather calmer man.

Leeds, with a longer route, showed better financial returns. Costs per mile, including interest and depreciation, worked out in the first few months at 6.3d while receipts were 10.75d. In the first nine months' operation, revenue totalled £1,508 and 229,641 passengers were carried. The cost of overhead in Bradford was £1,734 per mile against £1,240 in Leeds, a reversal of the estimates made earlier. This was because Bradford used span wires across the length of the road, thus requiring twice the number of poles.

A flood of inquiries followed the Leeds and Bradford openings, and many authorities visited the two routes. Among those interested but destined either to do without trolleybuses for years or not adopt them at all were Aberdeen, Bournemouth, Brighton, Chiswick, Dewsbury, Ealing, Edinburgh, Mirfield (near Huddersfield), Matlock, Newcastle, Northampton, Sheffield and Waltham Cross. Between 1907 and 1911 24 trackless bills were promoted, of which eight received sanction. In February 1911 alone there had been 15 bills before Parliament, five of them associated with the Railless company.

The visitors to the Yorkshire installations included the travel-tested deputation from Dundee, where a decision on trackless had been deferred after the 1908 continental inspection. The Board of Trade had raised no objections in the first place, and it was decided to equip a route along the Clepington Road from the Fairmuir district to Maryfield, a distance of a little over a mile. Two cars with Milnes Voss bodies were purchased at £700 each from RET. Opening day seemed auspicious. For on 5 September 1912, the British Association was meeting in the city, and 1,200 passengers were carried.

Soon, however, the two vehicles, numbered 67 and 68, were in trouble. The roads were hopelessly inadequate to sustain any regular passage of heavy, solid-tyred equipment. Existing potholes deepened, and whenever it was dry, the cars would drive through clouds of choking dust; the problem was so bad that they were nicknamed 'stouries' from the local word for dust, 'stoor'. By early 1913, after considerable wrangling, the tramways committee refused to meet the cost of maintaining the streets traversed by trackless. In fact, the system managed to keep going until 13 May 1914, by which time the damage to road surfaces was put at £6,000, the installation itself having cost a total of £3,000. The RET cars were stored until sold to Halifax at the beginning of 1918.

After World War I, Mr Fisher was asked by the technical Press to comment on a statement by a member of a Parliamentary Select Committee to a trade union official that trolleybuses were 'mostly failures'. The Dundee manager disagreed and said only the refusal by other Dundee officials to spend money on road improvement had caused the city's abandonment after 20 months of trackless service. 'The experiment was a complete success so far as the efficiency of the vehicles was concerned, and the financial results were quite satisfactory,' he told *Tramway and Railway World* in its issue of 14 August 1919.

Intriguingly, when delegates gathered in Dundee a month later for the annual Municipal Tramways Association conference, no mention was made of the trackless venture. It was usual for speeches of welcome—given in this case by the lord provost, the convenor of the tramways committee and Mr Fisher—to include a review of the host authority's transport achievements, and the omission of trackless was a surprise.

A month after the Dundee inauguration, another Yorkshire municipality set up a trackless route with the help of RET. This time it was Rotherham, which on 3 October 1912, put three single-deckers of Mr Munro's standard design on the rural route between Herringthorpe Lane and Maltby. It was destined to be the beginning of a system which kept trolleybuses for 53 years.

Another resourceful manager was in charge initially. It was usual for full twin-wire overhead equipment to be strung up only along the line of actual route. Getting to and from a nearby depot was usually achieved with the positive trolley getting current from the single tram wire, and a trailing skate going in the tram lines for negative return. The problem was that undue deviation from the tram rails would cause the skate to jump out. The Rotherham general manager, E. Cross, designed a pair of pony wheels about ten inches in diameter which were carried just in front of the trackless vehicle's front wheels. If the line of tramway had to be followed, the pony wheels would be lowered into the rail to guide the car as if it was a tram. Before leaving 1912, two important London trials should be mentioned. Early in the year, the London County Council, which owned a large tram fleet, experimented with trackless cars over the Woolwich-Eltham tram route. Overnight, the cars involved were stored at Abbey Wood depot. Presumably the vehicles were loaned by RET, which would have pulled off a considerable coup if it managed to arrange trolleybus traction in the capital so early. Little is known of the results of the LCC tests; it was to be another 19 years before trolleys appeared on London streets for regular farepaying passengers.

RET could not relax despite the early successes. The Austrian Cedes concern set up a British subsidiary in May 1910, to try and establish Cedes-Stoll systems. The first demonstration was at West Ham, London. A single-deck car which had seen service in Vienna was shipped over to be shown to delegates attending the 1912 Municipal Tramways Association conference. Greengate Street was equipped with Cedes overhead for $\frac{1}{4}$ mile, and the vehicle was run by West Ham Corporation for a week in September, even taking passengers. The blue and red single-decker was registered as A8DC, and could carry 24. The controller had seven positions: four series and three parallel.

Another development in 1912 was the promotion of an ambitious Parliamentary bill by Folkestone, Sandgate and Hythe Tramways, which wanted to operate railless traction and scrap tram lines authorised in Acts of 1906, 1907 and 1909. The proposal never became reality.

There was yet another collection system used on the continent, called Lloyd Kohler, or sometimes Bremen after the German city where it was first tried. Only one British authority adopted Lloyd Kohler, and that was Stockport. The two overhead wires were set vertically. A two wheel-trolley travelled on the top (negative) wire, and on the bottom ran a spring-loaded collector. This assembly was attached to the car by a flexible cable. Only one line of overhead was installed from St Peter's Square $1\frac{1}{2}$ miles to Offerton, so when two cars wished to pass, the cables had to be unplugged and exchanged. Three cars were purchased, being Daimlers with Brush bodies. They were smaller than RET's vehicles, seating only 20, and they were powered by a single 35 hp motor designed by Cedes Stoll. Operation began on 10 March 1913.

On 2 May, the country's first full-scale Cedes system opened at Keighley not far from pioneering Bradford. A route was equipped from Ingrow to Cross Roads, and Keighley acquired the West Ham demonstrator to inaugurate services. It was eventually numbered 0 in the Keighley fleet, probably a unique designation.

A conventional RET system was installed and ready for service at Ramsbottom on 14 August. Again Mr Munro's 28-seaters had Milnes Voss bodies, and front entrances. A 3 mile route was inaugurated from Holcombe Brook across town to Edenfield, planned presumably as a prelude to putting on the local authority's first tramcars.

Another trolleybus venture which could have been a reasonably-sized scheme was that mooted at Watford, Hertfordshire during 1913. Having staged the first trackless trial in 1909, Metropolitan Electric Tramways had been casting around for a suitable trolley route of its own and the company suggested the idea to Watford authorities as less expensive than trams in what was then a quiet far-flung satellite of London. A deputation went to the continent and among installations visited was the tortuous one beside Lake Como. Despite finding trackless cars a 'little clumsy' Watford was enthusiastic and it was suggested that a route be operated from North Watford to Bushey Heath. By the time firm plans appeared, war clouds were gathering over Europe and the actual start of war killed the project. The corporation engineer then was F. W. Purse, who 20 years later told a meeting of the Institution of Electrical Engineers that he thought Watford should have pressed ahead with trolleybuses.

War was eight months away when the first trackless system was opened in South Wales, Aberdare using Cedes-Stoll from 15 January 1914. It was a carefully thought-out project, being the first attempt to combine systematically railless and railborne transport. The proposals were steered through Parliament by a respected engineer, Stephen Sellon. His intentions were reported by *Tramway and Railway World* on the day trackless running began. 'There is no doubt that in the course of a comparatively short time the trackless trolley lines will have to be converted into tramways, and that the former will be re-erected further afield, thus forming one of those systems of light lines of which our continental neighbours have reaped the benefit for so many years past, and of which we have been lamentably in want.' Despite the verbosity the vision was clear and probably exactly right for the time. Eight cars were purchased with Cedes chassis and equipment and 27-seat Christopher Dodson bodies. Trolleys were towed to and from the depot at Gladlys by trams.

Hesitation on the possibility of installing a trackless system was still evident in Sheffield, which in 1909 had sent out the second continental deputation and later studied the Bradford and Leeds projects. Just before World War I, a Bradford car was loaned to the city for a week, complete with crew. Running under tram wire and with trailing skate, the vehicle was seen by delegates attending a tramway conference. Sheffield decided eventually on an extensive tram layout which was to be among the last in Britain to shut.

Down on the south coast around Brighton, trolleybus schemes had been brewing since 1910 when Brighton, Hove and Preston United Omnibus proposed a trackless route all the way from Worthing to Rottingdean with spurs northwards into the town centres of Brighton and Hove. The idea was viewed with horror by the local authorities concerned, and residents' support to fight off the company's plans was enlisted. They were urged to back a municipal trolleybus project, and ratepayers were shown a film at The Dome in Brighton in January, 1912 'showing Trackless Trolley Cars at work in Leeds and Brad-ford'. The next year both Brighton and Hove despatched representatives up north for first-hand examinations. By 1913, Brighton was ready to try out an RET car. It turned out to be the country's first double-decker, sanctioned by the Board of Trade in November. The open-topper boasted 40 seats, hydraulic suspension and two motors. Beginning on 28 December, the borrowed giant began the first of several trips with trailing skate from just south of Preston Circus along London Road to St Peter's Church. It was also tested on the quieter Ditchling Road, and a speed of 17 mph recorded. The on-the-spot observation of the *Brighton Herald* is worth quoting: 'To go along a road at nigh on twenty miles an hour, after the fashion of an inebriated person going home and visiting each side of the road with strict impartiality, is more like a ride on a switchback than a trolley 'bus. The greasy surface of the road made the ride none too safe either, and for any other driver to have pursued so erratic a course would inevitably have ensured his appearance before the magistrates.' The driver receiving such criticism was in fact the tramways manager, William Marsh! His passengers included on that occasion councillors and aldermen.

Their immediate impressions are not known, but representatives from Hove saw the trial, and were soon busy arranging their own. They were persuaded to experiment with the Cedes system, installing the peculiar overhead equip-ment from Hove station along Church Road. The overhead contractor was Clough Smith, which had carried out the installation at Aberdare and was starting on more than 50 years of trolley wiring. By arrangement with Clough Smith, Britain's second double-decker was borrowed, fitted with Cedes chassis and equipment and a Dodson body. Hostilities had started by the time of the first Hove trip on 16 September 1914. It appears that secrecy was intended, but contemporary photographs show plenty of intrigued bystanders. The blue and cream vehicle had only 32 seats, and with Cedes' Austrian parentage, the complications of wartime soon finished off the venture. Clough Smith was asked to remove the overhead, and it and the double-decker went to Keighley in 1916. The trial cost Hove Corporation £600 in out-of-pocket expenses for the dismantling of equipment.

RET was keen to develop its Cedes overhead work as well as offering under-running gear. In February 1913, young Alton Crosley, who had become Mr Munro's assistant two years earlier at the age of 21—another assistant who arrived early in 1914 was Charles Roe, who would go on to head the big Leeds bus building business of that name—was sent to Paris to see how Cedes-Stoll apparatus crossed over conventional tram wires. In the months running up to the declaration of war, much was still being learned from continental operators. By that fateful August of 1914, a mere eight systems were open in Britain, and not more than 25 trolleybuses were in use. Back in 1911, when the first two routes were equipped, there were already 33 trolley lines on the continent. About 100 vehicles were running over routes covering 200 km.

CHAPTER TWO

EQUIPMENT AND OPERATION

THIS century's world wars both came at crucial times in the development of public transport, shattering many ambitious dreams. The 1914-18 nightmare created tremendous problems for early trackless operators, mostly because the sources of equipment and technical knowledge turned out to be in enemy countries. Only two undertakings attempted wartime openings, and the first, Rhondda, was an utter failure. A study having been made of the Rotherham system, a $1\frac{3}{4}$ mile route with under-running current collection was opened in the Welsh valley three days before Christmas 1914. Six Cleveland vehicles with Brush bodies were used. The primitive road surface soon collapsed, and the system was closed the following March. It would prove to be the shortest-lived trolley service operation of all. The need had been to serve a colliery, and similar requirements led the Mexborough & Swinton company in Yorkshire to install a system in mid-1915, this time the basis of a network which would run for another 46 years.

When peace came, it was clear a wholly domestic 'trolley industry' had to be created. Edward Munro, the driving force behind RET, recognised this quickly. In September 1919, a catalogue published by his Bristol overhead wiring firm declared: 'Before the war, many of the fittings . . . were imported from enemy countries, principally because the selling organisation of firms in enemy countries was better than our own. We have in future to remedy this. . . .'

The ten years after World War I saw the new transport animals evolve away from mere tram route 'feeders'. The expressions 'railless' and 'trackless' were displaced almost entirely by 'trolleybus'. In fact the title still had strong tramcar origins, for 'trollibus' had come from the pioneer Virginia Railway and Power Company, and for Americans, the tram has always been a 'trolley'. Perhaps the most engaging definition of trolleybus was given in 1934 in *Bus and Coach* by Hampton E. Blackiston, then manager of the Ipswich system. He wrote that the vehicle was 'without doubt, the result of a combination of the electric tram and the motor bus. But there is a very great difference between a mongrel and a hybrid, the former being the accidental or uncontrolled mixing of two breeds, while the latter is the result of a careful selection and mating of two species which shall combine all the best attributes present in both of the originals.'

VEHICLE MAKERS UP TO 1939

The general development of trolleybus chassis manufacturers got an important boost in 1920 when the Ministry of Transport decided to relax the maximum vehicle weight from five tons loaded to five tons unloaded. This cleared the way for real development of the double-decker, and began the widening interest of established builders in trolleybus production.

Railless, as already seen, dominated the early market for vehicles, although the company did not begin producing its own chassis until 1922, a couple of years before it was entirely bought out by Short Brothers, with manufacturing facilities at Rochester, Kent. Until then, Alldays and Onions and Straker-Squire supplied most of the chassis for early networks, with the energetic Munro negotiating the ultimate terms with operators.

There was a close postwar relationship with Charles Roe's blossoming Leeds bodybuilding business, presumably a continuing link forged in the days when Roe had been one of Munro's assistants. Specially narrow vehicles with Roe bodies were supplied for York's small layout, and a dozen Roe-bodied trolleys for Birmingham in late 1922 represented the first large batch of double-deckers delivered to date. These carried English Electric motors, as did vehicles supplied in the next few months to Ramsbottom and Ipswich. From the mid-twenties, both chassis and bodywork were being produced at Short's Rochester factory.

By that time the Associated Equipment Company, much better known by the initials AEC, was making determined inroads, and the pioneers began giving way from 1926, when a repeat order from Birmingham for Railless arrived as Short-bodied AECs, the result obviously of a sub-contracting arrangement. The last Railless batch went to Nottingham for that town's 1927 inauguration; a repeat order shortly afterwards met with a refusal to name a price. Sadly, Railless never made a trolleybus with pneumatic tyres, although several undertakings did re-equip old solid-tyred vehicles.

The 1926 Birmingham order worked wonders for AEC, which had been formed in 1912, beginning trolleybus construction ten years later. Great interest was shown by the fact that 'non tram' builders were showing their faith in trolleys, and AEC found itself on the ground floor of a boom in demand.

Number of Vehicles in use

	Trolleybuses	Trams
1924-5	135	14,397
1925-6	191	14,434
1926-7	253	14,481
1927-8	319	14,403
1928-9	389	14,244
1929-30	492	13,922

AEC, and later its post World War II successor, British United Traction, really dominated the market. Numbers of units produced would eventually be overtaken by Sunbeam of Wolverhampton, but most of that company's trade came during and after the 1939–45 war. By the early 1930s, AEC's system of construction was established; three basic chassis were offered, numbered from 661T to 663T. At the 1939 Commercial Vehicle show, the 664T was to have been proudly unveiled, designed for a 74-seat body, but headed for South Africa where size regulations were less stringent. However, the outbreak of war led to cancellation of the show and indeed diverted such vehicles on to British streets, paving the way for larger public service vehicles generally, both electric and diesel-powered.

AEC stressed particularly the gruelling nature of the trials its chassis went through at the famous Southall works sited alongside the Great Western main line in Middlesex. There was an extensive test track on the premises, with gradients of one in nine. The booms were carried atop a 'box' of girder work extending 10 ft up from the chassis. Chunks of metal were placed on the chassis framework to represent passengers.

AEC's trolley vehicle design always followed to an extent its successful motor bus models. So in the mid-thirties, a Q type trolleybus on a special 761T chassis was produced, with bodywork and electrical equipment by English Electric. The main difference compared with current design was the positioning of the front wheels behind the front entrance line and the single rear wheels. The Q was ahead of its time, and only two were supplied to British operators, Bradford and Southend. The wheel arrangement proved the drawback, making the vehicle light at the back and hazardous to drive in icy conditions.

The fact that EE had built the Q body was by no means the first extension of the electrical group's trolleybus talents. It had made bodies since World War I, and from 1928 was designing chassis as well, usually subcontracting construction to Leyland.

Only one firm came really close to being able to boast of a complete trolley-

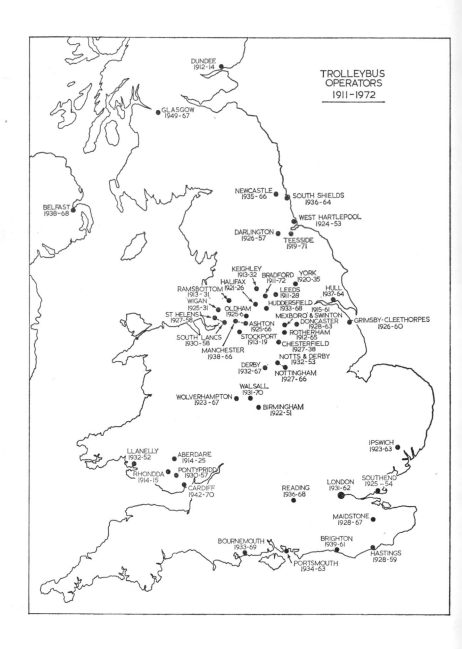

TROLLEYBUS
OPERATORS
1911–1972

DUNDEE
1912-14

GLASGOW
1949-67

NEWCASTLE
1935-66

SOUTH SHIELDS
1936-64

BELFAST
1938-68

WEST HARTLEPOOL
1924-53

DARLINGTON
1926-57

TEESSIDE
1919-71

KEIGHLEY
1913-32

BRADFORD
1911-72

YORK
1920-35

HALIFAX
1921-26

HULL
1937-64

RAMSBOTTOM
1913-31

LEEDS
1911-28

WIGAN
1925-31

HUDDERSFIELD
1933-68

1915-61

OLDHAM
1925-6

MEXBORO' & SWINTON
1933-60

DONCASTER
1928-63

GRIMSBY-CLEETHORPES
1926-60

ST HELENS
1927-58

ASHTON
1925-66

ROTHERHAM
1912-65

SOUTH LANCS
1930-58

STOCKPORT
1913-19

CHESTERFIELD
1927-38

MANCHESTER
1938-66

NOTTS & DERBY
1932-53

DERBY
1932-67

NOTTINGHAM
1927-66

WALSALL
1931-70

WOLVERHAMPTON
1923-67

BIRMINGHAM
1922-51

IPSWICH
1923-63

LLANELLY
1932-52

ABERDARE
1914-25

RHONDDA
1914-15

PONTYPRIDD
1930-57

SOUTHEND
1925-54

CARDIFF
1942-70

READING
1936-68

LONDON
1931-62

MAIDSTONE
1928-67

BOURNEMOUTH
1933-69

BRIGHTON
1939-61

HASTINGS
1928-59

PORTSMOUTH
1934-63

bus installation service, and that was Clough Smith, the overhead wiring business involved in trolley work almost from the start. In 1921, Clough Smith teamed up with Straker-Squire, supplier of many London motor buses and an early provider of trolley chassis, the first for Rotherham in 1912. The first Straker-Clough vehicles were single-deck 36-seaters for Teesside. An interesting point was the tyres: bone-jolting solids were falling into disfavour in the early twenties, and the Straker-Cloughs boasted tyres that were a cross between solids and pneumatics, then still very expensive. Another feature was the provision of electric braking on the rheostatic principle, with pedal control. Straker-Cloughs went to Darlington and Chesterfield in 1926 and 1927.

Clough Smith also formed a joint operation with Karrier Motors of Huddersfield. Karrier-Clough single-deckers, designated E4, went to York in 1931. The double-deck Karrier-Clough E6, popular in the early thirties, could carry 60 passengers up to 30 mph on a three-axle chassis. It could be lubricated, it was claimed, for less than a shilling a year. With both Straker and Karrier, Clough Smith acted only as the selling agent, not being involved in the actual manufacture.

Only a few years after the E6's introduction, Karrier was taken over by the Rootes Group in 1934. Construction work was transferred to Wolverhampton, home of Rootes' Sunbeam subsidiary, which had moved into trolleybus production in 1931 when it began publicising a six-wheel double-decker with Metropolitan-Vickers motors and usually Weymann body. Until the war, Karrier and Sunbeam vehicles were produced more or less separately, with little apparent standardisation of equipment.

Mention has already been made of the non-tramway origins of the early trolleybus builders, and this was never more true than with the Ipswich firm of Ransomes Sims & Jefferies, notable for its agricultural and horticultural equipment. It was appropriate that the company should have close links with the Ipswich town system, indeed the association between them was probably unique. In fact, Ipswich experimented first with Railless vehicles, but the authority purchased the first Ransomes trolleys from 1924 onwards.

The key figure in this partnership was Frank Ayton, an electrical engineer, whose career was typical of the pioneering commerce of late Victorian and Edwardian England. His numerous adventures included a 1,000-mile cable-laying expedition up the Amazon, after which he became responsible for the equipment of London's Waterloo and City electric railway, opened in 1898. It is significant that he was employed at the time in the London office of Alexander Siemens.

Mr Ayton was chief engineer of Ipswich Tramways from 1903 to 1921, and then joined the Ransomes board, where he seems to have wielded virtual control. In a catalogue published in October 1929, Ransomes boasted of being the only operator 'to make practically the whole of the bus in our own work-shops'. Ransomes made much of the fact its trolleys were *not* based on motor bus design. Originally, the firm offered three vehicle types: solid-tyred C and D trolleys, which were mostly single-deckers, and D6 six-wheelers, seating 40 if single-deck and 63 if double.

An occasion which provided some good publicity for both the company and Ipswich was the 1934 Royal Agricultural Show, held in the town for the first time. Ransomes was already involved because of its enormous range of farm machinery, but in a special brochure, it also spotlighted the locally-built trolleys. In five days, 95,935 out of a total of 107,234 visitors travelled by trolleybus to the showground, two miles out of Ipswich beside the London Road. Forty-six trolleybuses an hour were laid on, and the brochure was full of interviews with surprisingly articulate passengers from other parts of the country who were reported to have complained along the lines of 'Why our town doesn't install trolleys I'll never know . . .'.

Ransomes' trolleybus work was not destined to be of great importance, though, and only 500 vehicles were built up to 1939, half of them going abroad. In the mid-thirties, the practice of constructing the whole vehicle began to slip, several appearing with Brush bodies, for instance.

Still in Suffolk, another agricultural machinery maker, Richard Garrett and Sons of Leiston, was attracted by Ransomes' early success, and produced its own type S single-decker first shown at the 1925 Commercial show. Garrett was already experienced with electric battery vehicles for refuse collection, and so forth, but the same success was not to attend its trolley vehicles.

The original Garrett trolley was tried at Leeds, Keighley and Ipswich before entering service in Bradford. Experience with the S led to a modified O trolley-bus appearing. A six-wheel double-decker, type OS, appeared in 1927, having capacity for 27 passengers upstairs and 28 down. This was bodied by Garrett itself, with steel panelling and framework, although some other vehicles had bodies made by near-neighbour Ransomes or Roe of Leeds. Garrett seems to have been a prodigious supplier of demonstrators, but its trolleybuses mostly made up minor portions of individual fleets. The last of the company's 101 trolleys, a batch of O single-deckers for Mexborough and Swinton, were built in 1930.

Guy Motors of Wolverhampton had produced since its inception in 1914 a wide range of civilian and military vehicles. Innovation played an important part in all new models, and the first trolleybus, a three-axle double-decker for Wolverhampton in 1926, was the first to have pneumatic tyres. Motor bus design was the prevailing influence; the body was by Dodson, and regenerative brakes were fitted, always a feature of Guy trolleybuses. In 1935, anticipating postwar regulation changes, Guy designed a chassis capable of taking a 30 ft long body, and such vehicles went overseas as exports flourished. Early Guy trolleys had Rees-Stevens electrical equipment, but by 1939, the firm was designing its own motors.

Of all the manufacturers hit by World War II, Leyland, the famous Lancashire commercial vehicle group, seemed to suffer most, with at least one important order, from Cardiff, being diverted to a peacetime competitor because of Government orders to switch to war work. The first Leyland trolley had appeared in 1927, and after several demonstration trips, went into service in Bradford in 1929. A batch of Leyland trolleys was ordered for Birmingham in the early 1930s, and the firm was a big supplier when London Transport began ordering trolleybuses in large quantities. Altogether Leyland as an independent trolley builder turned out 1,400 vehicles, but many went abroad.

Daimler of Coventry, better known of course for sleek motor cars, was involved in trolleys early. It had linked with the Brush bodybuilding concern to supply three Lloyd Kohler cars to Stockport in 1913, and Daimlers made up the first Mexborough and Swinton batch in 1915. Another interesting link-up came in 1926 when AEC and Daimler formed the joint Associated Daimler company for sales purposes. Only seven vehicles came of the marriage. They were all single-deckers, equipped with Bull motors, and went to Bradford as the city's first pneumatic-tyred trolleys. One lasted almost 20 years, although for the last seven it was a grit wagon. Nothing more was built until the CTM4 and CTM6 chassis were offered in 1938.

In 1931, Crossley Motors, based in Manchester, had produced its first diesel-engined bus, but was a latecomer to the trolley market. Its first vehicle appeared in 1936, a demonstrator shown off in Ashton under Lyne. Nearby Manchester put on trolleybuses two years later, and chose the local Crossley firm to supply a large part of the fleet.

VEHICLE MAKERS AFTER 1939

The need for fighting equipment during World War II, a conflict so much more mechanised than the 1914-18 war, swiftly curtailed work on civilian vehicles. By 1942, the Ministries of Supply and War Transport were sanctioning only one chassis builder to produce trolleybuses—the Sunbeam and Karrier business at Wolverhampton. The authorities stated that the firm had a design 'suitable for all', and so the famous Sunbeam-Karrier W4 chassis appeared all over the country.

It was a two-axle design, and the traction motors were positioned rather lower than usual to permit low-bridge bodies to be fitted without major structural changes. The motors were normally 80-85 hp, and were supplied by four well-known electrical companies: BTH, English Electric, Metropolitan Vickers, and General Electric. The standard austerity bodies came from three sources: Weymann, Park Royal, or Brush.

Return to normality for trolleybus builders came in 1946, the year when AEC and Leyland merged their trolley interests into British United Traction, and BUT and Sunbeam were to satisfy most of the postwar demand.

In the main, AEC built those double-deck BUT vehicles intended for the home market, while Leyland chassis for single-deckers went abroad. Postwar designs from both sources generally provided for either 7 ft 6 in or 8 ft wide bodies. The first BUT chassis was designated 9611T, superseded after 1952 by the 9641T, basically the same but with a longer wheelbase. Leyland BUTs did enter service in Britain—an RETB/1, a revolutionary 'standee' vehicle, going to Glasgow in 1951, followed by another ten in 1952. The next in the BUT series, 9612T, was produced at the Manchester factory of the absorbed Crossley concern, 70 such vehicles going to the local Manchester and Ashton system. Thanks to the efforts of R. Edgley Cox, manager at Walsall, 30 ft long chassis with two axles were permitted in the mid-fifties, and BUT chassis were built to this specification for Glasgow and classified 9613T. Also delivered to the city were 34 ft 6 in single-deckers on RETB/1 chassis. Ten were purchased in 1958 and were BUT's last home order.

Guy resumed production in 1947, supplying 70 three-axle trolleys to Belfast and 50 two-axle types for Wolverhampton. In September 1948, the Sunbeam Trolleybus Company was absorbed, and the name Guy no longer appeared on trolleys.

Sunbeam eventually built just over 1,600 trolleybuses for home and overseas. Its domestic chassis postwar were the MF2B, the F4, the F4A, and the S7. Sixteen MF2B vehicles, with Roe bodies and dual entrances, went to Hull between 1953 and 1955. Bournemouth took delivery of the last batch between 1958 and 1962; no 301 which entered service in November, 1962, being Britain's last new trolley. This chassis, the ultimate offered in domestic trolleybus design, was 30 ft long with two axles; the wheelbase was 15 ft 10 in long giving a 65 ft diameter turning circle. The Weymann bodies fitted had an aluminium panelled exterior—with the exception of the vulnerable lower offside panel made of fibre glass. There was an open rear entrance and a front exit with folding doors beside the driver. Seating was for 63. Crompton Parkinson provided the 95 hp motors. The F4A was the chassis which in 1955 became the first to boast two axles on a 30 ft long frame. Fifteen entered service that year in Walsall, with Willowbrook bodies seating 70 plus automatic acceleration. Another seven followed the next year. The S7 was 3 in short of 30 ft and was a three-axle chassis. Huddersfield took delivery of a batch in the late fifties which were Britain's last new six-wheel trolleys.

As for Daimler, it found two postwar customers: it supplied part of the 1949 fleet for Glasgow, the last British trolleybus undertaking to open; and was responsible for 46 single-deckers for Rotherham with 38 seats apiece. In the late fifties 20 were converted to double-deck.

TRACTION EQUIPMENT

As with chassis and bodywork, motor design remained relatively crude until the 1920s, when liberalising of weight regulations was followed by an upsurge in demand. Early railless vehicles often had two hub motors, each driving one rear wheel. The equipment, subjected to intense vibration as the solid tyres travelled over the road surface, tended to be unreliable, and as already pointed out, World War I often sealed off the sources of replacement parts.

When double-deck trolleybuses began appearing in quantity, motors were usually twinned on a common armature shaft with series-parallel operation. Controllers tended to be of tramcar type; in the first place drivers had to juggle with a steering wheel and hand controller, but foot control was an obvious advantage and was universal from the mid-twenties.

Another ten years saw the introduction of the single traction motor, and such equipment was standard after the outbreak of World War II. Trolleybus electrical gear had to cope with arduous traffic conditions, with frequent stops and starts, and to allow increased current to the motors for acceleration, electrical contactors enabled weight to be kept down to the lowest level compatible with the necessary performance. Operation of the compound motor was arranged with both series and shunt field windings. The motor started off with full shunt field and all the main starting resistance in circuit. Step by step, the starting resistance would be cut out, and then further acceleration to a balancing speed as high as 37 mph depending on motor size could be obtained by weakening the shunt field which eventually was wholly de-energised.

Electric braking represents one superb advantage of the trolley—and to a lesser extent the tram, for that matter—over the motor bus. Regenerative braking tended to be popular initially, although because its application returned current to the overhead line system, elaborate protection equipment was necessary on both vehicles and substations to prevent voltage overloads. Regeneration worked by reversing the master controller over a part of its travel to strengthen the shunt field. The motor regenerated the motion of the vehicle into electrical energy, braking the trolley and returning current to the line. The regeneration would be effective down practically to walking pace when the driver had to apply the air brake for a final stop. Writing about trolleybus braking towards the end of the last war, G. H. Pulfrey, general manager at Hull, observed that the needs and experience of operators varied greatly: 'Some state that with the use of regenerative equipment they obtain substantial power savings, but this will, to a great extent, depend upon the particular locality. In Hull, where the going is absolutely level, the saving on this account is very small.' London, with its huge fleet, was to find regenerative equipment highly convenient.

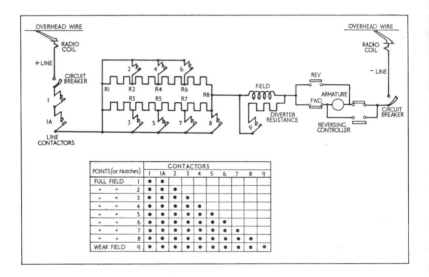

POINTS (or Notches)	CONTACTORS									
	I	IA	2	3	4	5	6	7	8	9
FULL FIELD 1	●	●								
" " 2	●	●	●							
" " 3	●	●	●	●						
" " 4	●	●	●	●	●					
" " 5	●	●	●	●	●	●				
" " 6	●	●	●	●	●	●	●			
" " 7	●	●	●	●	●	●	●	●		
" " 8	●	●	●	●	●	●	●	●	●	
WEAK FIELD 9	●	●	●	●	●	●	●	●	●	●

Simplified method of operation, and order in which line and resistance contactors close during acceleration. (Eight running positions and one weak field)

Overvoltage relays had to be installed in regenerative trolleybuses, which, if operated, would disconnect the power supply and establish rheostatic braking. In later years, a form of limited rheostatic braking for overall use became more popular. Application of one or two steps of rheostatic while the vehicle coasted would turn the motor effectively into a generator. By feeding the power created back into a portion of the main starting resistance, a trolley could be braked down to a few miles per hour. This sort of equipment was perfected by English Electric, which originally called it the series-dynamic brake. Urging operators to install rheostatic brakes, manufacturers would warn of the perils of regenerated electricity affecting both traction and other roadside installations.

Trolleybuses were pioneers in the use of air brakes, which in normal conditions on practically all vehicles after the mid-1930s, were only needed to reduce speed under 5 mph. Electric braking, therefore, prolonged the life of brake liners. In 1952, the dramatic effect on tyre wear too was illustrated in figures prepared by W. J. Evans, then Reading's manager, who was arguing the merits of electric braking for motor buses.

	Tyre life
Motor buses	Fronts: 32,000-38,000 miles
	Rears: 15,000-18,000 miles
Trolleybuses	Fronts: 52,000-53,000 miles
	Rears: 73,000-75,000 miles

The advantages were not all one-sided: Mr. Pulfrey noted that some operators complained of oil loss from rear axles because of the heat created during electric braking. He thought the savings in brake liner removal alone compensated for this.

Activation of the contactors was made through a master controller, incorporating both the accelerating and braking equipment; and a most important feature was the interlock provided so that the switch to reverse the vehicle could not be moved unless the controller was in the off position.

One item of equipment that always caused problems never completely solved was the resistance grid. The need was for ample resistances to absorb the heat produced during acceleration and braking, yet achieving this within the required weight was a knotty business. By their nature, resistances tended to be fairly fragile, so they had to be mounted in a sheltered position—but at the same time, a free passage of air was needed to provide enough cooling. Various manufacturers tried different locations. In some respects, single-deckers, despite their low seating capacity, provided the ideal solution: resistors could go on the roof. After World War II, resistances tended to be made of stainless steel, freeing operators from worries about corrosion.

The electric power characteristics of a trolleybus allowed the use of two pieces of safety equipment: runback and coasting brakes. The first was to prevent a vehicle running backwards out of control. A special contactor would be energised and held open during ordinary running. If the vehicle was dewired, or the power failed or there was a voltage overload, the contactor would open and limit the speed backwards to about 2 mph.

Much the same function was performed by the coasting brake, except that its use was a conscious act by the driver. In certain towns, before descending a steep hill, regulations demanded that the trolley be stopped and the driver move the controller switch to the 'Coasting Brake' position. The series winding of the motor was then brought into action, bringing the vehicle under ordinary rheostatic brake control and limiting the forward speed to 12-14 mph.

Trolleybuses were embarassingly dependent on the overhead wire. Traction batteries could be a useful means of emergency propulsion, yet there was always a lively debate between operators on the relative merits. Again, the contemporary observation of an expert sums up the argument. E. T. Hippisley, traction sales manager of BTH, was quoted as saying in 1936: 'It appears to be the opinion of the majority of provincial operators that the additional cost and dead weight of (traction batteries) are unjustifiable for their conditions of service, and in general these operators find no difficulty in securing adequate space for turning points at route termini or at intermediate points.' The last comment was obviously a reference to the situation in London, where all vehicles carried batteries because it was sometimes awkward to provide adequate overhead installations at congested termini. If fitted, batteries could provide enough power to move a trolleybus for up to three miles at low speed on a level roadway. It became the practice to run low voltage lighting inside and outside a vehicle off batteries, rather than direct from the overhead. But such batteries operated in parallel so one fault would not affect the whole circuit. If emergency propulsion was required, heavy-duty batteries would be operated in series with the throwing of a switch in the driver's cab.

On the subject of cab equipment, another important item was the circuit breaker. Its function was to trip out the electrical equipment if too much voltage was passed through the motors. Also, in the event of a short circuit, the opening of the breaker would protect other trolleybuses in the same section. If the breaker switch opened, the driver could attempt to re-close it, although power would only be restored permanently if the fault was temporary. In the early days of trolley operation, trailing skates were often used to allow vehicles to run with the positive boom on a single tram wire, the current return being made through the skate into a tram rail. A U-shaped box was provided behind the driver's head to shift control from the negative boom to the skate.

The first trolleybus fitted with automatic acceleration appeared in Nottingham in 1945, although English Electric had patented equipment so designed seven years earlier. This enabled the driver to concentrate on road and over head conditions, and usually obviated the need for overvoltage relays, since current peaks during speed build-up were dictated by the equipment. Depressing the power pedal either near or to its full range would ensure smooth acceleration, graduated according to gradient. By 'feeling' his way through the pedal's path, a driver could still 'notch up', but jerky starts were prevented. There comes a point, of course, where rate of acceleration becomes too great for passenger comfort; the highest rate for British trolley undertakings was eventually 4 mph per second up to 20 mph.

The capacity of motors grew steadily. In 1919, 20 hp was common. In 1928, it was 100 hp; 1939, 115 hp; and after 1945 the need to design equipment for 'transit' trolleys abroad led to motors capable of 150 hp. The following figures give an idea of the best performances put up by the most modern trolleybuses used in Britain in the fifties and sixties.

	Maximum speeds		
On a level road:	Empty	42	mph
	All seats taken	38	,,
	'Crush loaded'	35.5	,,
1 in 7 gradient:	Empty	20.2	,,
	All seats taken	18	,,
	'Crush loaded'	17.2	,,

The drive towards standardisation meant that after 1945, electric motor manufacturers tended to market a set range of motors suitable for broad variations in local conditions. Metropolitan Vickers, for instance, offered three motors. The MV 209 with standard winding developed 103 hp and was suitable for vehicles up to 12 tons laden operating in level conditions; the MV 210 with standard winding (125 hp) was for similar weights but hilly roads; and the MV 210 with high speed winding (135 hp) was for vehicles up to 14½ tons on hilly routes. The manufacturers emphasised the low maintenance costs of a trolleybus and the reliability of the traction equipment. In 1946, English Electric carried out a special test, sealing up the control motor switches on a vehicle which was put into constant service. Fifteen months later, practically no wear was reported when the equipment was opened up.

A determined effort was made after 1945 to create the sort of boom in trolleybuses which had followed World War I. In 1947, Metropolitan Vickers staged a three-day conference to bring together manufacturers and operators to talk maintenance and design. It may have been a neat way of pushing the products of Metrovick, which supplied most of the equipment for London's

1,800-strong fleet, but it also represented a philosophy of expansion, temporary though it would prove to be. Subjects covered included 'Maintenance of control equipment' and 'Development in relation to performance.' More interesting was the time devoted to 'Planning new projects.' There were to be only a few, unfortunately.

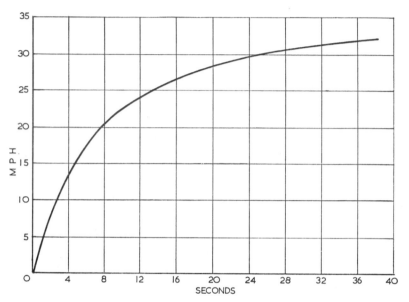

Trolleybus acceleration (Early 1930s)

THE OVERHEAD

To be slightly illogical, the trolleybus would have been fine without the overhead paraphernalia. Two major problems were obvious right from the start: the tangles of wire in town centres were unsightly, and the system itself denied trolley vehicles vital flexibility. In later years, the need to modify traffic flows in congested urban areas exposed the weaknesses of a practically perm- anent traction layout. The point was recongised by one of the first trolley operators in Britain, Bradford's Christopher Spencer, who in the mid-thirties suggested that radio transmission of power could overcome dependence on street wiring.

The requirements for the overhead were more or less based on tramway practice, and had the same essential aim—to prevent dewirements. Until the last war, when several shoddy layouts had to be modernised because of black-out regulations, dewirements were due as much to poor installation as bad driving. The run of the wires, with the negative nearest the kerb and normally two feet from the positive, ignored minor irregularities in the kerb line to ensure smooth running. On roads up to 26 ft wide, the negative wire could be no more than seven feet from the side; up to 11 ft was allowed with roads having a maximum width of 45 ft. Span wires strung right across the road between traction poles were preferred for carrying the running wires. Single metal bracket arms needing poles on one side of a street only were permissible as long as they did not exceed 16 ft. Initially, where the roadway was over 40 ft wide, bracket arms were required on both sides. Curves had to be arranged so that the radius of the wire was less than the normal route of a vehicle, and installations like turning circles had to be equipped with adequate street lighting. The minimum height of wires above the ground was 20 ft, although less was allowed under bridges, where strict speed limits applied. Supporting wires or arms could be no further than 120 ft apart, although 105 ft was generally used. As far as the actual wire was concerned, all early systems used copper, but from about 1930 onwards, cadmium-copper alloy became popular. The alloy was more hard-wearing, although its conductivity was slightly lower. The postwar standard wire had a cross section of 0.125 sq in. Running wires were suspended from spans by a hanger, a unit with a spacing bar plus two 'ears' and two insulators.

If trolleys were to succeed trams on a particular route, existing poles could often be used. In 1934, one manager reckoned that reinforcing existing equipment cost only 34s against a new pole at £7 10s. Whether new or old, poles had to be sunk to a minimum depth of 6 ft. The total length of a pole, including the part below the surface, could vary from 31 ft to 40 ft. A treatise on overhead installation published in 1939 cautioned transport managers against having flowery coats of arms, scroll work, or other ornamentation on poles because such devices tended to hasten corrosion. Tramway operators had always shown a penchant for street decoration.

A curious warning to fellow managers was given by T. P. Sykes, general manager at Rotherham. 'It is essential that the wire shall be maintained at one standard height from the surface of the roadway,' he wrote in *Bus and Coach*. 'If left to their own devices, linesmen may measure the position of bracket arms from the top of the pole, and as it is never certain that all poles are carried the same depth in the ground, this method may lead to large variations in the height of the trolley wire, which at high vehicle speeds tend to (cause) dewirements even on straight wire.'

For restricted sections under bridges, each trolley wire could be clamped to a steel T-section 'backbone' supported from the bridge structure by porcelain insulators. Often, more simple wooden troughing clamped only at each side of the bridge was used. Regulations stipulated that the clearance between the underside of a bridge and the vehicle boom had to be not less than 12 in. There had to be at least seven feet between the bridgework and the top deck of uncovered vehicles run by the early operators. With all applications to vary measurements because the restrictions could not be met, the Ministry of Transport declared that 'each case will be considered on its merits.'

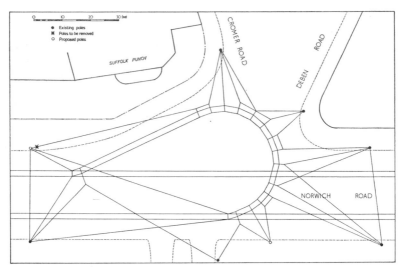

Wiring contractor's detailed plan for a typical turning circle
Courtesy A. G. Ratcliffe

Curves in overhead wire were originally obtained by inserting 'pull-offs' which were additional span wires allowing the running wire to deviate up to ten degrees from the straight. In later years, the curve segment made its appearance, holding the wire in a smooth continuous arc, the metal frame being of galvanised steel. The segments allowed curves of up to 45°, and cut down wear and dewirements at corners. By reducing the number of extra wires, they tidied up the overhead; another important advantage was that segments were prefabricated before installation, cutting down complicated work 'in the air.'

At a maximum spacing of $\frac{1}{2}$ a mile, section insulators had to be installed, allowing current to be switched off in convenient stretches in emergency. Ideally, the insulators had to be on a straight length of road to avoid dewirement. As far as the wire running surface was concerned, there was a 12 in break filled by a strip of insulator, constructed with the same profile as the adjoining wire to prevent damage to collection gear.

Railway points became 'frogs' in overhead wire parlance, and there were two types: hand-operated and automatic. In the first case, a sprung steel pull cord ran through a pole adjacent to the frog. The handle would be at convient hand height, and if pulled as the trolley booms were passing would swing over the tongues for the diverging movement. Automatic or electric frogs were perfected before the World War II by an American concern, the Forest City Electric Company of Illinois. To move from the main to a branch line, a trolleybus would draw current when passing under a setting skate inserted in the overhead wire. This would energise a solenoid, which in turn set the point tongues for the turn-out. As the vehicle entered the branch section, the collector head would come into contact with a striker wheel to reset the frog through a connecting link. Vehicles were limited to five miles per hour through frogs, and as traffic densities increased, driving trolleys to suit pointwork at busy road junctions became difficult. So the interlaced frog became more popular. The actual turn-out would be sited some convenient distance before the junction, and once diverged, the two sets of wires would run parallel until the point of separation. To inform drivers on the setting of frogs, lamp indicator boxes were provided at junctions, with bidirectional illuminated indicator strips. The boxes were normally $8\frac{1}{2}$ in deep, with an anti-glare hood over the indicators.

Special hazards were presented by the proximity of other wires, and the precautions to be taken rested with the trolleybus undertaking, as made clear in a typically comprehensive Ministry of Transport directive of 1938. It stated: 'If and whenever telegraph, telephone or other wires unprotected and with a permanent insulated covering, cross above, or are liable to fall upon, or to be blown on to, the overhead conductors of the routes, efficient guard wires shall be erected and maintained at all such places.' Overhead wiring changed relatively little in the 61 years of commercial trolleybus operation, although later installations tended to look 'cleaner' as the apparatus was modernised. The shadow of traffic congestion made turning circles and reversers at termini increasingly dangerous, and in the fifties and sixties, termini layouts were sometimes arranged by putting wires up round suitable layouts of back streets.

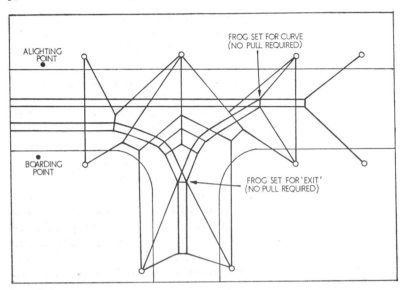

Overhead wiring for reverser at terminal lacking space for a turning circle

As for the vehicles themselves, connection with the overhead was made by trolley heads bolted on to the one-inch diameter booms down which the wiring travelled. Immediately beyond the boom was a metal 'harp' on which sat a swivelling gunmetal globe. Following tramcar practice, trolleybuses were originally fitted with trolley wheels running along the wire. These were generally four inches in diameter, although larger sizes were tried to reduce dewirements. A non-trolleybus authority, Edinburgh, was the first to try carbon skids in its tram collectors instead of wheels, and mostly because of the significant decrease in wire wear, they became widely adopted. Officials at Bradford reckoned that using skids raised 'wire life' from 8 or 10 years to 15 or even 20 years. Many experiments were done to try and determine the best length of carbon insert, which fitted into a bronze 'slipper' on top of the globe. In consistent weather conditions, a skid lasted about 800 miles. One worn skid could damage the overhead, in turn wearing out carbons on other vehicles using the same route. Changeable weather meant a much reduced carbon insert life. In extreme conditions, like that on Hastings' long, exposed seafront route to Cooden, maintenance crews would sometimes have to fit new skids to vehicles during the few minutes' layover at termini. To ensure efficient collection, the pressure of the trolley head on the wiring had to be fairly high, al-

Page 53. (*right*) Cedes collection equipment on an Aberdare car in 1914, while (*below*) a conventional RET car turns at a bleak Rams-bottom terminus

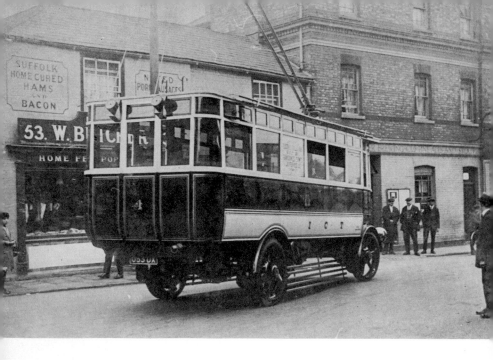

Page 54. (*above*) Ransomes' car for Ipswich, 1924. Note trolley retrievers. (*below*) Singledeck and open-top Guy double-deckers in early Hastings scene

though the actual amount varied widely. For instance, Bradford was content with 38 lb, but London insisted on 48 lb. The pressure exerted had to be checked regularly by hanging a scale from each boom, kept in position by a stirrup. Another important test, which had to be done daily, involved checking the insulation of the electrical conductors from the vehicle's metal work. Ministry regulations required a trolley to be taken out of service if the reading was above three milliamps.

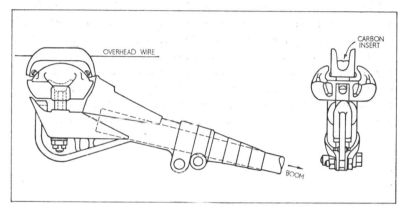

Carbon insert trolley collector
Courtesy: Brecknell, Willis

The cost of cadmium-copper wiring became very high after World War II. In the late 1950s, the annual cost of maintaining one mile of overhead was put at £7,500. Most maintenance work was done by crews using tower wagons, and it was reported in one technical journal that by 1953 13 undertakings had short-wave radio to keep in contact with overhead staff. A number of special tools was available to adjust the overhead, including a 'straightener,' described by the manufacturer as a 'compact and portable tool for straightening the kinks or bends unavoidable when erecting trolley wires.' It was pushed along the wire by means of geared rollers.

The overhead for numerous trolleybus schemes was put up by Clough Smith, which from just before World War I until the mid-sixties was electrical contractor for most projects not tackled by authorities themselves. Constructional engineer A. G. Ratcliffe joined the firm in 1929 and stayed for 40 year to take charge of most of the work, travelling all over the country as new systems were installed. He recalled that after the 1932 Derby scheme, Clough Smith only just survived a lean period until Portsmouth put on trolleybuses in 1934, then contracts were more or less continuous. The last big scheme was the rewiring of Belfast's central area in 1958, and Clough's last trolley job of all was in Cardiff in 1965 in connection with the St Mary Street one-way system.

REGULATION AND ARGUMENT

The tram was an obvious relative of the railway train, and the trolleybus was related to the tram. So it was that trolley systems had to endure the yoke of being treated by the authorities as light railways. This meant obtaining full-blown Acts of Parliament for new routes, and even for extensions. In later years, when trams were practically forgotten, the curious legal position of trolleys was to cause at least one rumpus. During World War II, the Ministry of Transport inspecting officers, who devoted most of their investigating powers to railways, authorised some towns to equip new routes before obtaining the necessary powers. After the war, authorities keen to extend trolley routes successfully obtained special powers allowing them to fill the gaps in existing networks. One advantage was enjoyed because of trolleys' special status: schedules and other internal matters could be arranged without interference from the area traffic commissioners.

It appears that civil servants had tried before 1914 to free trolleybuses from cumbersome legal provisions, but had encountered powerful opposition. This battle was revealed by Sir William Marwood, Joint Permanent Secretary to the Board of Trade, in evidence to the House of Commons Select Committee on Transport in February 1919. He recalled that in 1912, the Board of Trade had endeavoured to take powers to authorise trackless trolley systems when it had a 'small act' before Parliament for amending the Light Railways Act. The move was defeated in Grand Committee. Sir William blamed the 'good deal of opposition' on the County Councils Association. Its objection was understandable—several big towns were planning to extend trolleybuses into country districts, and experience at the time was showing how rural roads were damaged by the new vehicles. On the other hand, new tram routes required rails which tended to strengthen road surfaces. The county authorities were afraid that without the opportunity to argue cases as Bills were going through Parliament, unwanted trolleybus systems would spring up.

Trolleybuses' anomalous position meant that early vehicles required no road fund licences. These became necessary under the 1920 Finance Act, and registration plates had to be carried after 1921. Still, there were some privileges: in

March 1952, when anything except semaphore indicators were illegal, there was nothing to prevent Bradford trolley number 758 from becoming the first vehicle to use flashing indicators lawfully.

The great transport debate of the late 1920s and the 1930s revolved around the rival merits of trolleybus and motor bus over the declining tramcar. The high cost of imported oil and the desperate need to keep jobs going in the collieries gave the trolleybus a distinct edge. A relatively small number of important operators, including Liverpool, Leeds, Edinburgh, and until after the second war, Glasgow, pressed on with trams in great numbers.

Those keen on the motor bus were made to feel almost anti-social. After the angry period of the General Strike and the slump, a director of the Electric Development Association asked 'was it right' with high unemployment, to use buses in place of trams 'run by electricity, in generating which, much coal produced by the miner (is) needed.' Figures rained down. It was estimated that replacing all trams by buses would mean the consumption of an extra 87 million gallons of oil a year. Trolleybuses had longer life, few moving parts, and, proving that 'environment' and 'pollution' are not entirely creations of the supersonic age, they were quieter and produced no foul fumes. Wolverhampton, the first town to use six-wheel trolleys, plucked out figures showing they were

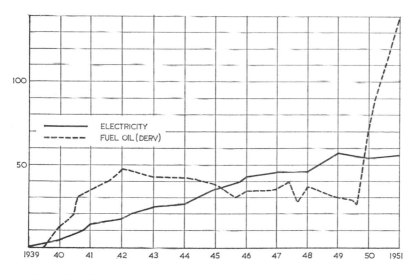

Relationship between prices paid for electricity and fuel oil 1939–51 [Based on: *Electricity* 0.587d per unit paid by traction undertakings in 1938–9; *Fuel Oil* 1/1½d per gallon in August 1939]

faster too: trolleys' average speed including stops was 9.436 mph, around 1930, against 8.607 mph for the bus. Financial incentives were there: the Ministry of Transport was allowing authorities ten years for repayment of trolley installation loans in the early thirties, against seven years for buses.

Apart from manoeuvreability, the trolleybus offered other significant advantages over the tramcar. Christopher Spencer, who as already noted, only wished the overhead could be replaced by getting energy to the vehicle by 'some radio power transmission scheme,' reported that London United Tramways' early vehicles had cut current consumption by 18 per cent. A man with a reputation for stern dealings with his staff, Mr Spencer also remarked that being easier to drive, trolleybuses could be run by cheaper labour. He was speaking at a joint meeting in May 1933, of the Institution of Electrical Engineers and the Institute of Transport, when he also suggested that 'trackless' and 'railless' grated upon the nerves, and he urged the complete adoption of 'trolleybus.' In modern terms, he was concerned at the image of the trolleybus, which was certainly becoming an important element in street transport. Figures produced elsewhere for the financial year of 1929-30 put the trolleybus in a fine light. (All have been converted to new pence):

	Trolley	Tram	Bus
	p	p	p
Average revenue per mile	6.14	7.12	5.11
Average operating expenses per mile	4.55	5.53	4.42
Fuel cost per mile	0.73	0.8	1.05
Gross profit per mile	1.69	1.5	0.89

Among Mr Spencer's audience was Assistant Commissioner H. Alker Tripp of the Metropolitan Police, who during a lively post-address debate said that trolley turning circles were a source of concern to the police. He was also doubtful about the relative safety of larger trolleybuses. He would have been reassured no doubt by some statistics unearthed by another early authority on the trolleybus, R. A. Bishop. He claimed that fatal accidents to those using trolleys and trams amounted to only 0.0244 per million passengers.

Still on the subject of image, the editor of *Bus and Coach* argued in October 1933, that motor bus design should not influence trolley builders: 'In his search for the ideal trolleybus the designer would do well to free himself of many motor bus chassis conventions which may hinder rather than help him in his work.' It is instructive that 19 years later, the magazine was inveighing against manufacturers who were keener to satisfy the demands of overseas markets than those of British operators. The result was that the horsepower of motor equipment was 'higher than is necessary for home conditions. Whereas 60-80 hp is probably sufficient, 95 to 120 is being advocated.'

The heart of the matter was the changed circumstances postwar, causing argument not just on the merits of trolley versus bus, but on the survival of trolleys at home at all. The British Electrical and Allied Manufacturers Association took up the cudgels, issuing leaflets stressing the trolleybuses' advantages. At the end of 1951, the association claimed that 'confusion' about overhead costs was weakening the case for the trolley. Wild estimates that a mile of double track overhead would cost £11,000 led to an investigation. The answer: a figure of £5,340 was found to cover materials and construction. Operators were urged to take advantage of the regulations allowing traction poles 120 ft apart rather than the generally-adopted 105 ft.

Later, the association broke into verse, apologising as it did so to the author of the wider-known original:

> 'The Chairman and the Manager
> Were watching workers stand;
> They wept like anything to see
> Such queues on every hand.
> "If only these could ride away,"
> They said, "it would be grand."

> "If seven queues in seven lines
> Waited for half a year,
> Do you suppose," the Chairman said,
> "A bus could get them clear?"
> "I doubt it," said the Manager
> And shed a bitter tear.

> The Chairman and the Manager
> Were trying day by day
> To cut down cost of maintenance
> and make the system pay.
> They wondered if the trolleybus
> Might be the better way.

"The time has come," the Chairman said,
"To talk of many things,
Of costs, and fares, and oil supplies,
Of pumps and piston rings,
And why the engine's boiling hot
and how the fuel tax stings.

"I really think," the Chairman said,
"The trolleybus would do
Just what we want. Its excellence
Our profits would renew."
The Manager just smiled and said,
"I'm thinking that way too!"'

Battling on, the association claimed in 1956 that staff records showed drivers employed on trolleybus operation were more likely to be long-serving.

DRIVING

Mechanically, the driver of a trolleybus had on the whole a simpler job than this counterpart behind the wheel of a motorbus. Yet the need to watch conditions overhead as well as on the road demanded special skills. When trolleybuses were delivered to Brighton, the following instructions were issued to drivers, and they form a typical description of conditions elsewhere:

Commencement of day
When the vehicle was brought into the depot from service, the circuit breakers and other switches should have been opened before the trolleys were lowered from the line.

In taking the vehicle into service therefore the driver should establish the power circuits by switching on in the following order:

1. See that the circuit breakers are open, and all switches are in the "OFF" position.
2. Place the trolleys on the overhead wires.
3. See whether the trolley dewirement indictor is alight.
4. Close the compressor and control switch.
5. Close the circuit breakers.
This will start the compressor. If the air pressure is low, it will be necessary before moving the vehicle to wait until the operating air pressure has been reached. A buzzer is usually fitted to indicate low air pressure.
6. Set the reverser handle to the appropriate position.

Starting

The smoothest start is obtained by applying the first notch of power *before* releasing the handbrake.

After striking the first notch, release the brakes and allow the bus to start moving. It will be found that on the level all but the heaviest loaded bus will start on the first notch. Then feed through with a uniform pedal movement.

It is not necessary to try to find each notch in turn as the notches will take care of themselves if the driver keeps the pedal moving smoothly downwards.

The driver will however be able to tell the notching by the slight noise of the closing contactors.

When starting on up grades, depress the pedal slowly and gradually release the handbrake after striking the first notch. After the bus is felt to move take the next few notches more slowly than on the level in order to allow the bus to accelerate without tripping the overcurrent relay or circuit breakers.

The second or third notch will usually start the bus on the steepest grades.

Motoring

The first nine notches are main resistance notches and any prolonged running on these notches will overheat the resistances.

On the tenth to thirteenth notches however, the driver can run for long periods without creating difficulties.

These are the notches on which to regulate the running speed, and after a little experience the driver will have no difficulty in picking them out.

Stopping

1. Service stops.

Release the power pedal.

The bus will coast a considerable distance, according to conditions, without undue loss of speed. The power pedal can, therefore, be released some distance before the desired stopping point, thus reducing energy consumption.

Next depress the brake pedal until the first notch of rheostatic braking is obtained. As the bus decelerates the brake pedal should be further depressed to introduce the second notch of rheostatic braking and, when required, still further to introduce air braking and finally bring the vehicle to rest, when the handbrake should be applied. A partial release of the brakes immediately before the bus comes to rest will give smooth jerk-free stopping.

In normal circumstances, as soon as the handbrake has been applied the brake pedal should be released in order to open the circuit to the motor shunt field and the shunt field resistances.

During normal service stops on the level the rheostatic braking will reduce the speed to 3 or 4 mph before it is necessary to introduce the air brakes for finally stopping.

On the steepest down grades rheostatic braking will reduce the speed to 5 or 6 mph.

If, after having applied rheostatic braking, it is then desired to accelerate, release the brake pedal and depress the power pedal. The power pedal should be depressed quickly past the first few notches in order to take up the driving torque immediately and thereby avoid a check to the bus.

On steep down grades both steps of rheostatic braking, and, if required, air braking as well, may be applied simultaneously.

2. Emergency Stops.
        Apply the air brake as quickly as possible.

Section Insulators

1. When approaching a section insulator, switch off smartly by releasing the power pedal.
2. After the trolleys have crossed the gap, switch on again smartly to the same position of the pedal.

Coasting Brake

See that the controller reverser drum is fully moved into the 'coasting brake' position. This is important. In this position it will be felt that the handle springs into a gate so that it cannot inadvertently be knocked out.

The bus must be at rest when the 'coasting brake' position is either engaged or disengaged. Burning out of the reverser drum will ensue if this instruction is disregarded.

Brighton vehicles were always rheostatically braked. Instructions for regenerative braking would have told the driver that, having notched up with the left-hand pedal, lifting the foot would notch back and bring in various steps of regeneration, slowing the trolley to a few miles per hour. The right foot operated the air brake, either for emergency stops or for the final stop. Among the practical points of operation, drivers found that automatic acceleration equipment, when fitted, performed slower than manual notching up.

POWER SUPPLY

Current supplied for trolleybus traction varied between 500 and 550 volts dc. Most substations were unattended, housing high tension ac switchgear and mercury arc rectifiers, connected to the overhead by short feeders. The rectifier units were usually of the glass bulb type. Compared with trams, pneumatic-tyred trolleybuses drew a high amount of current during acceleration, and the equipment had to be specially tailored to suit this need. Automatic trip gear had to have high settings. On systems using regenerative trolleys, the voltage load could rise to 900, and the substation equipment had to allow staff to distinguish normal traction 'peaks' and faults. The average consumption of electricity per trolleybus was reckoned at 3 kWh.

The number of passengers carried and vehicle usage reached a peak in 1950, and the accompanying table shows how the situation developed outside London:

	Vehicles	Passenger journeys (Millions)	Receipts (£ mill.)	Vehicle miles (mill.)
1937	1,559	497	2.85	47.23
1949	2,322	1,110	7.83	79.15
1950	2,321	1,115	8.19	80.54
1951	2,212	1,077	8.57	77.65
1952	2,168	1,019	9.10	74.94
1953	2,060	980	9.28	72.53
1954	2,001	946	9.16	70.23
1955	1,952	914	9.18	68.29
1956	1,892	877	9.53	66.34
1957	1,853	839	9.96	64.34
1958	1,828	785	10.11	63.40

Comparison is provided by figures for London Transport between 1953 and 1958:

	Vehicles	Passenger journeys (Millions)	Receipts (£ mill.)	Vehicle miles (mill.)
1953	1,797	747	9.2	74
1954	1,764	717	9.3	71
1955	1,764	684	9.5	65
1956	1,614	631	9.9	64
1957	1,585	604	10.5	63
1958	1,536	477	8.5	52

CHAPTER THREE

LONDON

THE figures at the end of the last chapter show that London carried about three-quarters the number of passengers as the rest put together. As the capital, it had by far the largest trolleybus fleet, but trolleys never played more than a secondary role in transport policy; it was only 13 years after their introduction that a virtual 'death sentence' was passed, even though it was to be a lingering death. The roots of this unenthusiastic approach lay in the composition of London's transport authorities. Until the thirties these comparised the tram-dominated London County Council, the London General Omnibus Company, various small companies and local councils. None seem to have the resources and inclination to trackle trolleybuses on the scale of the reasonably-sized provincial centres.

Of 49 trolleybus systems in Britain, London was the 32nd to open. The plunge was taken in 1931 by the London United Tramways, associated with the Underground group and consequently the LGOC, which operated services in south west London. The company had got a reputation for forward-thinking, gained from the thrusting personality of an early manager, James Clifton Robinson, who had died in 1910. As World War I ground to a halt, a new character appeared on the scene, auguring well for eventual trolleybus development. Christopher Spencer, who had begun trolleybuses in Bradford, became manager of the LUT from 1 November 1918. As already seen, London trolley schemes had been mooted before that, but the first postwar plan centred on Richmond Bridge, in LUT territory. In 1922 the LUT borrowed for trials a double-deck front-wheel drive colossus which had been built by Trackless Cars Ltd of Leeds and shown at that year's tramway operators' conference in Bournemouth. In November 1923, a Bill was presented for the conversion to trolley operation of a route from Richmond Bridge to Twickenham, with the wires going on to Fulwell, the depot where the Trackless double-decker had been tested. Vehicles would have turned in quiet side roads near the bridge, and this seems to have become the focus of opposition. At any rate, the route was left to buses run by the General group.

Not far away, and in the previous year, the South Metropolitan company, which operated trams in the Croydon, Mitcham and Sutton districts, tested a single-deck under-running trolley in the Anerley area. It was thought to have been one of Bradford's 'second generation' RET-type cars of the 503-20 series. The single tram wire plus a trailing skate were used. The trials were somewhat marred by an accident on 10 February when a cyclist was killed in a collision involving the trolley. An LCC proposal for a West Norwood-Lee Green trolleybus service met so much opposition that it was abandoned about this time. LUT conducted other trials, and in that summer a second wire was strung up between Summerstown and Queens Road. At the latter terminus, children who helped push the trolleybus round for the return trip were given free rides, becoming the first London trolleybus passengers south of the Thames.

Nothing solid came of the experiment, however, and no more progress was made until LUT formulated its plans for the 1931 opening. From comments made when several trolley proposals were under discussion, it looked as though the Metropolitan Police were less than keen on trolleybuses: tramcars may have been a nuisance by making passengers swarm into the road at stops, but at least trams did not swing round in a circle at the terminus.

LUT's proposals were embodied in a Bill presented to Parliament and approved in 1930. Basically, it gave the company powers to convert to trolley-bus operation any of its routes clustered round the Twickenham-Kingston-Tolworth line running from north to south. Wiring was in position between Twickenham and Teddington before the end of the year. Sixty trolleys were ordered in the first place, all on AEC chassis and with Union Construction Company bodies—both AEC and Union Construction were associated with the Underground group and consequently with LUT. The first 35 had English Electric 80 hp motors, the remainder, 82 hp equipment supplied by BTH. They were six-wheelers and could accommodate 24 passengers downstairs and 32 up. The balancing speed was reasonably high for the time at 29.4 mph. After they had entered service, a large single, tram-style headlight was fitted on the 'bonnet' and these distinctive vehicles were used until 1948. Their nickname of 'Diddlers' has produced all sorts of explanations as to its origin. Remembering how much quieter they were than trams, I favour the theory that the name came from about the only noise that was distinguishable—that of the equipment notching up during acceleration.

The Twickenham-Teddington stretch was finally opened by the Mayor of

Twickenham on 16 May 1931, a month and four days short of 20 years since the Bradford and Leeds ceremonies. LUT trolleys number 4 and 5 were suitably decorated and ran to Fulwell depot where there was a celebration lunch. On 5 June it was the turn of the Mayor of Kingston to inaugurate services in his area. Eventually Twickenham, Kingston, Tolworth, The Dittons, Hampton Court and Wimbledon were covered by four basic routes with the most frequent services operating on a five-minute headway. Most of Fulwell depot was occupied by trolleys, and it is interesting that the premises were still divided into 'tracks,' tramway practice which seemed to persist with trolley operators all over the country. The conversion of $17\frac{1}{4}$ miles cost £230,000, and the new vehicles generated 26 per cent more revenue. Costs were reduced by 13 per cent overall, with current consumption down 18 per cent, according to the statement already noted from Mr Spencer at a 1933 conference. His desire to get rid of the old terminology was reflected by the roadside descriptions ... passengers waited at the 'Trolley 'Bus Stop.' One problem by no means confined to the LUT was that of radio interference created by trolleys. The solution approved by Mr Spencer, that of fitting choke coils to the vehicle roof behind the trolley base, was copied elsewhere. Before the LUT passed out of existence, it did introduce one 'modern' trolleybus to add to its fleet: number 61, an AEC, carried a London General body and English Electric regenerative equipment. For the public, the noticeable thing was that no. 61 had a 'full fronted' look with a cab going all across the front of the lower saloon. One 'un-London' feature, however, was the centre entrance.

The London Passenger Transport Board took over inner and suburban road services in July 1933, its only trolleys being LUT's 61 vehicles. One of London Transport's chief preoccupations was the replacement of the huge tram fleet, and trolleybuses seemed the obvious choice. The first move was to decide on the most suitable vehicle, and two experimental trolleybuses were delivered in 1934. Following on with the LUT classification system, no. 62 was designated in the X2 class. Another AEC, it had Metrovick equipment. No. 63, classed X3, was similar except it was the only four-wheeler ever used in London. Both were withdrawn in 1952, LT having plumped for the three-axle 70-seater as its basic trolleybus requirement.

The path was not going to be smooth, however. The rickety trams had one important advantage: in the central area unsightly wires were unnecessary because the cars used conduit pick-up. The 1928 Royal Commission on Transport which had preceded the important 1930 Road Traffic Act had doubted whether trolleybuses would ever run in central London. Controversy surfaced in the correspondence columns of *The Times* with a letter from 12 distinguished members of a London conservation society, London Transport had earlier published proposals for trolleybus routes, and the thought of long-ago battles going to waste with the appearance of wires in the inner area horrified the conservationists. They deplored the 'vandalism' planned for Bedford Square, and called the concept 'highly dangerous.'

In fact, trolleybuses would be consolidated first in the suburban areas, where the rapid spread of semi-detached villas required cheap public transport as the trams disappeared. LT's first route was an 'in-filling' job in the old LUT district. On 19 October 1935, routes were opened from Hammersmith to Hampton Court and Shepherds Bush to Hounslow. As well as the existing trolley depot at Fulwell, another was sited at Hounslow. The next month, the focus switched to a completely new area, south east London. The isolated Woolwich, Bexleyheath and Dartford services, originally operated by the Bexley, Erith and Dartford tramway undertakings were converted to trolleybuses, becoming routes 696 and 698. This section always remained cut off from the overhead elsewhere. The depot was at Bexleyheath, and for overhaul vehicles were towed to Charlton works. Later, when routes were converted to trolleybus operation opposite Woolwich on the north side of the Thames, trolleys would be loaded on to the free ferry, and then transferred to Charlton. In December 1935, the old Southmet tram route between Sutton and West Croydon became trolleybus 654. Two months later, trolleybuses ran on to Crystal Palace via the notoriously steep Anerley Hill. Partly to operate this route, LT introduced classes B1 and B2, which were 66 Leylands with Metrovick equipment. They had short wheelbases for hilly, tortuous routes. Three of them from Sutton depot, later called Carshalton and home of the 654, were fitted experimentally after World War II with transmitters to try and perfect radio operation of frog-changing. Two long aerials swept down from the roof across the front of the trial trolleys, looking rather like outsize whiskers. Also being introduced between 1935 and 1937 were the C1, C2 and C3 classes, 250 standard-length AECs with English Electric traction gear.

Meantime, route conversion was going on apace. The remaining LUT tram routes and western services of the former Metropolitan Electric Tramways were changed to trolleybuses in 1936, and at the end of the year, another part of London got its first trolleys when the Manor House-Woodford route was converted. The following year, London Transport began sweeping the tramcar out of east London; the same year tackling the remaining West London routes in earnest. These were the first ex-LCC tram services to be axed, 25 years after the LCC had dabbled with trolleybuses with the Woolwich-Eltham experiment. In 1938, routes in Ilford and north London were switched to trolleybuses, and trolleys got to Highgate in 1939. The outbreak of war probably prevented one last important area from getting trolleybuses: those suburbs due south like Camberwell, Brixton, Streatham, and so forth. The final district to see trams replaced was the Commercial Road in east London, converted on 8 June 1940.

Building of new London trolleys was a rolling programme from 1936-7. Four Leyland B3s arrived in 1936. The D class were Leylands with Metrovick equipment, and 160 were delivered up to 1937. Next, for east London schemes, came the E class, 98 AEC vehicles with English Electric motors. No. 622, an E2, sported a plaque reminding customers that it had been the first trolley fromWest Ham depot. Appropriately, it was selected as the last into the depot when it closed in 1960. The F1 class was a batch of 100 Leylands, and 150 similar trolleys arrived in 1938 as the H1. The J class swung back to AEC again, 147 being delivered in 1938. The K1 and K2 were 200 Leylands which entered service in 1938 and 1939. The alternating principle worked again, with the 173 L class being delivered by AEC in 1939 and 1940. However, the practice changed with the 120 trolleybuses classified M and N because these too were AEC. The last Leylands designed for London were 25 K3 in 1940 and 25 P1 in 1941.

Sandwiched between the regular batches of vehicles were a variety of experimental vehicles, most of which did not fulfil London Transport's expectations. This was not entirely true of X4 class no. 754. Basically a joint project between LT and AEC, it was the first trolleybus constructed by London Transport, being assembled at Charlton. The revolutionary aspect of the vehicle was the fact it was based on a chassisless unit, an approach widely adopted in subsequent models. LT also decided to study passenger flow techniques by installing a front exit door, but that was later sealed up. No. 754 operated from Finchley depot. Trolley no. 1379, classed X5, was designed to make use of one tremendous asset exclusive to London's trams—the Kingsway subway. This speeded cars underneath the busy Holborn and Aldwych areas, with intermediate tube railway-type stations. The subway came into the open to the south underWaterloo bridge on the Embankment.With its tram conversion programme in full swing, London Transport decided to try and run trolleys in the tunnel, and 1379 was suitably adapted. An offside folding door was installed at the rear for the underground island bays. Run-back and coasting brakes were fitted because of the steep ramp at the subway's northern approach. During darkness on 13 August 1939, two test trips were made without mishap. Power was provided by extra traction batteries, brake pressure being maintained by large portable cylinders. Two months before, specially-posed pictures complete with pretty girls had appeared in the Press showing 1379 with both entrances open and a special destination board announcing 'KINGSWAY.' Apparently, the clearances in the subway were sufficient, but LT was still trying to work out the problems of current collection—the trams, of course, used the convenient conduit—when war came and snuffed the plan out. After tramway abandonment, it was not until the late sixties that part of the tunnel was finally re-opened as a useful, if only uni-directional, link for all sorts of traffic. Another unusual animal in 1939 was no. 1671, designated X7. This was a Leyland demonstrator acquired by LT, its feature being the four-wheel front steering. The idea was not adopted, although the vehicle lasted until 1956, the year 'Kingsway 1379' also went to the scrapyard.

One trolleybus class is missing from the records. The G1 was to have been a batch of single-deckers for use on the service to Alexandra Park in north London. The plan for such a route never materialised, and neither, incidentally, did a scheme to equip a tube line to the same destination, branching off the Northern Line. The service was subsequently covered by bus route 233.

During the difficult days of 1941-3, London's trolleybus fleet got an important boost with the introduction of 43 vehicles which had been built by AEC and Leyland and intended for South Africa. The danger of losing the vehicles in submarine attacks at a time when space on ships was at a premium anyway meant their allocation to London. Other towns received similarly diverted trolleys. They replaced early London Transport losses, and enabled the capital in 1941 to return some of 18 trolleys borrowed from Bournemouth. The 25 Leylands were classified SA1 and SA2 and had GEC motors; the 18 AECs with English Electric equipment became SA3. The vagaries of wartime introduced to British streets a type of vehicle not previously allowed, for the chassis was 8 ft wide, instead of the usual 7 ft 6 in. They were equipped for front exits, a facility not used in London. Those vehicles which had been headed for Durban had smoked glass in the top half of the windows to ward off the African sun, a humorous touch for vehicles destined to spend their life operating from Ilford depot around the murky streets of the East End. In fact, as with other trolleys, windows blown out in air raids were sometimes boarded up. The SA classes lasted until scrapping between 1956 and 1960.

Trolleybuses in London took a lot of punishment during the air attacks of World War II, with 17 vehicles being completely destroyed. However, the relatively simple construction of a trolley meant there was usually scope for rebuilding a damaged vehicle. Three firms were involved in rebodying a total of 61 trolleybuses, and those attended to carried a distinguishing suffix letter after the original number. Those rebodied by Weymann carried 'A', East Lancs Coachbuilders 'B', and Northern Coachbuilders 'C'. Sixteen trolleybuses were rebodied in 1941-2. The most serious incident of all occurred during the 'doodlebug' campaign, when a VI flying bomb exploded at Bexleyheath depot on 29 June 1944. Out of the wreckage, 26 trolleys were recovered and reconstructed. Earlier, during the blitz, when improvisation was all-important, trolleybuses managed to defy their 'inflexible' description when bombing brought down overhead wires and blocked streets. At least three times, temporary new wiring was strung up to get trolleys round stricken areas. On other occasions, trolleybuses would be towed for short distances when the overhead had been wrecked.

Whatever the short-term emergency achievements of the trolleybus, London Transport took the fateful decision in 1944 that further tram replacement would be undertaken with motor buses. The implications were obvious, and every other authority in Britain was soon forced to think about the long-term feasibility of the trolleybus. Actual trolley replacement in London on a comprehensive scale was in fact still 15 years away. The postwar period was soon, dominated by the need to trim public transport costs and increase efficiency and from March 1945, trolley no. 61, the old LUT's unique vehicle, was converted to pay-as-you-enter. It was not single-manned, though, and the conductor was seated at a desk. The vehicle operated on the 604 Hampton Court-Wimbledon service. A similar experiment was instituted with C3 class no. 378.

The long-term plans for trolleybus replacement envisaged leaving the south west area with the form of traction it had introduced to London. The problem was the 1931 Diddlers were coming to the end of useful lives, and partly to replace them, London Transport ordered its last batch of new trolleys. Its prewar suppliers, AEC and Leyland, had merged their trolley-making activities into British United Traction, and so 127 BUTs entered service between 1948 and 1952. The first 77 went to Fulwell to take over from the LUT originals which had been classified A1 and A2. The BUT trolleybuses were classed in sequence as Q1, although there was no relationship with the 'Q' type front entrance vehicles tried in Bradford and Southend before the war. The Q1 was not to last long; many were sold to Spanish operators in 1961. Two were converted to motorbuses in Bilbao.

There was a flickering in 1950 of the mass withdrawals to come, when as part of the new conversions of tram routes to buses, trolleybus service 612 between Battersea and Mitcham was withdrawn. Converted at the same time

Page 71. (*above*) Modern L3 class with London's first passenger service trolleybus, LUT no. 1. (*below*) Cheers for West Ham's 1937 inauguration

Page 72. (*above*) An example of London rebodying after war damage is this Leyland with Weymann body—originally it had Metro-Cammell. (*below*) Busy Holborn in 1952, with Kingsway subway experimental vehicle in the centre

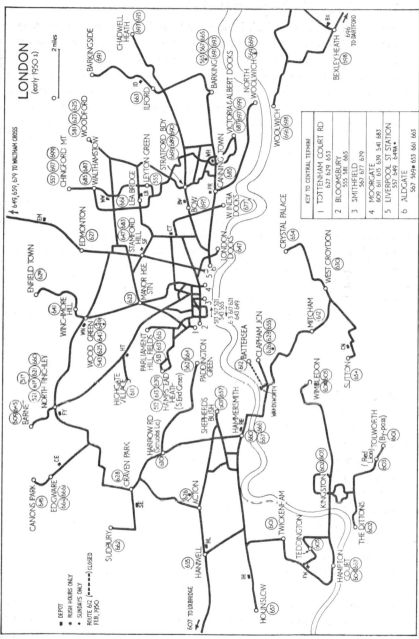

LONDON
(early 1950 s)

2 miles

KEY TO CENTRAL TERMINI

1	TOTTENHAM COURT RD 627 629 653
2	BLOOMSBURY 555 581 665
3	SMITHFIELD 567 677 679
4	MOORGATE 609 611 615 639 541 683
5	LIVERPOOL ST STATION 557 549 649A •
6	ALDGATE 567 569 653 661 663

■ DEPOT
* RUSH HOURS ONLY
* SUNDAYS ONLY
ROUTE 612 (▪▪▪▪▪) CLOSED
FEB. 1950

H.B.T.B.—E

was Wandsworth depot which housed the 86 trolleys used on the route. In fact the decision only resulted in two miles of overhead being dismantled at the Battersea end. Most of the route shared wires with the 630. Apart from 'losing' the 612, the network of London's trolleys stabilised in the mid-fifties with 64 basic routes which tended to be in loose groupings according to areas. Ten of the services were in the 500 series, and those stayed north of the Thames. The first four partnered routes in the 600 series, a break with normal London Transport practice: for instance, the 517 ran from North Finchley to Holborn Circus, and the 617 operated in the reverse direction round the terminal loop. LT has a strong policy of using suffix letters to denote subsidiary routes, but this was seldom seen on trolley services. An exception was the 649A, which paralleled the 649 from Liverpool Street Station to Tottenham, branching off there to Wood Green while its 'parent' made the longer trip to Waltham Cross. Half a dozen of the 25 or so night services run by London Transport were on trolleybus routes, but here again LT practice altered as far as trolleys were concerned: night buses tended to carry special route numbers, but all-night trolleys usually operating part of their daytime journeys would carry normal numbers. The conservationists of the mid 1930s won most of their battles, for trolleybuses never seriously penetrated the central area, terminating at fringe points like Holborn, Bloomsbury, Smithfield and Tottenham Court Road.

A universal policy applied to crew training, and a high standard was demanded for all drivers. What was probably a unique piece of training equipment was installed in 1937 at the Stonebridge Park school for trolleybus men. It was the brainchild of the inventive R. Edgley Cox who crops up at several stages of trolleybus history, making a mark in most places. While working for London Transport he devised the equivalent of a flight simulator to acquaint drivers with the procedure for notching up and, because LT used regenerative trolleys, notching back. The trainee sat in a full-scale mock-up of a driving cab. Beside him was the contactor gear. As he depressed the 'power' pedal the notching sequence showed up on a board in front of him. Similarly, the breaking sequence was illustrated. The idea was to show the driver how movement of his foot corresponded to performance, and which notches he should avoid lingering on because the current was in a resistance phase.

The grand conversion of London's trolley system began in 1959, lasted three years, and cost a hefty £10.5 million. The first withdrawals were in January 1959 with the closure of routes 664, 683 and 695, one in the north west, the second in the north, and the other eastward. In all cases, these services duplicated existing ones, so no wiring disappeared. On 4 March came the first of the 14 proper conversion stages, each aimed at taking about 100 trolleys off the road.

First to go was the 654 Sutton-Crystal Palace and the 696 and 698 tucked away in North Kent. The plan was to supplant trolleybuses with new Routemaster buses, but a shortage of these at the right time led to the apperance on replacement services of ordinary RTs. The following five stages in 1959 concentrated on trolleybus routes east of the Lea Valley. Stages seven and eight in 1960 saw the disappearance of routes in west London and on Highgate Hill, and the next three steps encompassed north London and the central area, or as near to it as trolleys were allowed. In January 1962, the north west district was 'cleared' and London Transport turned its attention to the original stronghold in the south west. Originally, LT had expected to continue trolleys in that area until the 1970s. The postwar QIs were rather heavy on current, and it was realised they ought to be sold while the vehicles had some decent value left. So older trolleys took over routes based at Fulwell, and their replacement could not be long delayed.

The official last day was 8 May 1962. One Diddler, no. 1, had been preserved at the Clapham transport museum in South London, and it was brought out for the day, making a trip from Fulwell via Twickenham to Kingston, loaded with local dignitaries and LT officials. The last trolley of all crept into Fulwell depot early on 9 May. No. 1521, a C3 class first run in 1940, had worked the final duty on route 604.

At their peak, trolleybuses covered 253 miles of London streets, and the fleet reached a size of 1,811 vehicles. The financial pressures obviously turned against the trolley vehicle in the metropolis, but is notable that, apart from 1951 when losses were incurred because of wage increases, trolleybuses were the only form of London transport profitable in the difficult years between 1948 and 1953.

DEPOTS

Name (Some changed in Oct., 1950)	Code (Introduced Oct, 1950)	Routes*	Capacity	Converted
Acton	—	607, 655, 660, 666	—	26.5.37 †
Bow	BW	661, 663, 695	102	18.8.59
Bexleyheath	BX	696, 698	75	3.3.59
Colindale (formerly Hendon)	CE	645, 664, 666	48	2.1.62 †

DEPOTS

Name	Code	Routes*	Capacity	Converted
Carshalton (formerly Sutton)	CN	654	51	3.3.59
Clapton (formerly Hackney)	CT	555, 581, 677	90	14.4.59
Edmonton	EM	627, 649, 659, 679	122	18.7.61
Fulwell	FW	601, 602, 603, 604, 605, 661	120	9.5.62
Finchley	FY	521, 609, 621, 645, 660	108	2.1.62
Hammersmith	HB	626, 628, 630	65	19.7.60 †
Hanwell	HL	607, 653, 655	108	8.11.60
Highgate (formerly Holloway)	HT	513, 517, 611, 613, 615, 617, 627, 639	230	25.4.61
Ilford	ID	691, 692, 693, 695	34	18.8.59 †
Isleworth (formerly Hounslow)	IH	657	37	8.5.62 †
Lea Bridge (formerly Leyton)	LB	581	33	14.4.59 †
Poplar	PR	565, 567, 569, 665	149	10.11.59
Stonebridge Park	SE	626, 628, 660, 662, 664, 666	86	2.1.62
Stamford Hill	SF	543, 643, 647, 649A, 683	97	18.7.61
Wandsworth	—	612	86	30.2.50
West Ham	WH	565, 567, 569, 665, 669, 685, 687, 689, 690, 697, 699	170	26.4.60
Wood Green	WN	623, 625, 627, 629, 641	108	7.11.61
Walthamstow	WW	557, 623, 625, 685, 697, 699	107	26.4.60

* General allocation for depots open 1954.
† Closed.

CHAPTER FOUR

THE SOUTH AND EAST ANGLIA

ALTHOUGH London was relatively slow off the mark, a handful of towns in the South and East had already installed trolleybuses, the first being Ipswich in 1923. Some of the systems served seaside resorts with a good deal of holiday traffic, and thus were very different from routes in the rest of the country which tended to cluster in gritty industrial centres.

One of the first extensive replacements of tram services by trolleybuses took place in this Suffolk market town, but not until a large body of opposition to the idea of continued electric traction had been defeated. The state of the tram installations forced a decision on the Ipswich authority in the early twenties, and it was decided to try a relatively cheap experiment. Three Railless cars were delivered for a route which was just 0.625 mile long. The vehicles were single-deck and one-man-operated, and they were hardly a stunning success. Mechanical failures were frequent, and so were dewirements. As passengers' ire increased, a whispering campaign developed, and motor buses found many supporters. In 1924, the local Eastern Counties Road Car Company offered to take over Ipswich's transport system and run buses. Yet, as we have seen earlier, the influence of Frank Ayton, the former Ipswich manager who had been a director of Ransomes, Sims and Jefferies since 1921, was no doubt being exerted, and instead of accepting Eastern Counties' proposal, the town purchased its first Ransomes trolleys in 1924. They were single-deckers, and the trolley bases had the booms mounted one above the other.

As services expanded more Ransomes trolleybuses followed, and vehicles also came from the other Suffolk agricultural machinery maker diversifying into passenger transport, Richard Garrett of Leiston. Ipswich's first fleet of double-deckers sported the slogan 'Ipswich electricity is cheap' on the front

77

beneath the cab window. The method of traction was also emphasised in the name of the central terminus, Electric House, where trolleybuses turned in a large square. The detractors were soon shown to be undue pessimists: in the first full financial year, trolleybuses earned a gross surplus of £839, which had improved by 1933-4 to a net surplus of £2,469. During World War II the rickety overhead was reconstructed. German air raids were a nuisance, and incomplete lengths of new overhead had to be sufficiently well erected to be left in emergency, still leaving wires for trolleybuses to run. So the contractors strung up the replacement overhead above the old wiring. The fleet grew in size, eventually totalling over 125 trolleys, housed in depots at Priory Heath and Constantine Road, which was an old tram shed. The town stuck to a 'trolley only' policy until 1950, and at that time was still running antique Ransomes trolleybuses purchased around 1930. The system ended without ceremony on 23 August 1963, when no. 114, a Park Royal-bodied Karrier F4, worked the last service, the 6.36 pm from Electric House to Priory Heath on route 2. Transport employees festooned the vehicle with a few decorations, and 'R.I.P.' appeared on the sides.

SOUTHEND

A similar start to that at Ipswich was made by Southend-on-Sea, which on 16 October 1925, inaugurated an experimental service from Victoria Circus to Prittlewell using two single-deck Railless cars on hire. A year-and-a-half later, the corporation began building up a modest fleet, starting with a double-deck Garrett, then moving on to English Electric, AEC and Sunbeam trolleybuses.

In the mid-thirties the system took delivery of two unusual trolleys. In 1934 it purchased a unique four-wheel centre entrance trolley, the only one to be produced by the Gloucester Railway Carriage and Wagon Company, which was numbered 122. Southend also operated an AEC Q type, as already noted. The fleet size eventually reached 38, which after 1945 included single-decker Leylands purchased from Teesside and secondhand Sunbeams from Wolverhampton. To the day tripper, Southend was not obviously a trolleybus town, as very little wiring reached the sea front. Trolleys were killed off by a transport phenomenon which, as we shall see, closed several other systems. In this case, it was an agreement with the Eastern National bus undertaking which put town services under co-ordinated management after 1953. Trolleybuses seldom found a place in such arrangements, and in October, 1954, the last trolleys ran on the western circular route, which had needed only seven vehicles to keep going.

HASTINGS

In this rather upper middle class community we encounter the first of the provincial company-owned trolleybus networks. Hastings Tramways decided on a six-month trial of trolleys in 1928, equipping a route from Hollington to Fishmarket via the doubtfully-named Bohemia area. The first eight vehicles were old-fashioned from the start, being open top Guys with Dodson bodies. They turned out to be successful tram replacements, and before the end of the year, wires had reached the next-door resort of Bexhill. The fleet was expanded at first with single-deck Guys, and this collection of vehicles was to soldier on unaided until 1940. The service to Bexhill was pushed out along the lonely coastline to Cooden, a low-density housing area which has still not become really developed. The trolleys were infrequent there, as they were on a circular route in Hastings itself where there was a 40 minute interval between trolleybuses, probably something of a record then. It was clearly a penny-pinching system, and the original general manager, W. Vincent Edwards, was known as a martinet with an unforgiving nature. Old employees remember he installed meters in the trolley cabs to see which drivers 'wasted' electricity, and demotion to conductor was the penalty for heavy users of current. It was not long, however, before the men had a ruse to answer this threat—on the long, lonely trip to Cooden they would switch over the booms and run the dreaded meter back to a respectable figure!

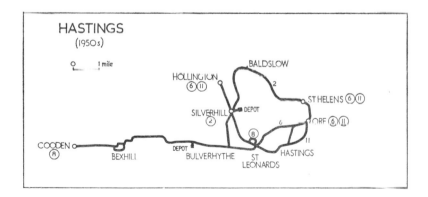

In 1935, Hastings Tramways became a subsidiary of the Maidstone & District group, but about the only changes were the replacement of the maroon livery with green and cream and the co-ordination of respective services. To take the place of the first Guy trolleys, AEC and Sunbeam double-deckers were ordered just beforeWorldWar II and some were delivered in 1940. The unsightly overhead offended some citizens, the local authorities reflected their feelings, but negotiations with M & D came to nothing. The company's powers to run trolleybuses were opposed in vain before a House of Commons committee, but a concession was won so that the boroughs of Hastings and Bexhill could purchase the network after 1945. The urge to do so was always there, but fate stood in the way. In 1945, Hastings council decided to go ahead with purchase, but the vote was found to be invalid. In 1950, the economic position forced a 'no' decision, but in 1954, the town's transport committee voted in favour only to have the full council throw the resolution out because of financial difficulties again. Too late, attitude began to change; in 1955 the Hastings Chamber of Commerce called for a new trolleybus service from the Silverhill district westwards towards Bexhill, and support was forthcoming from the Hastings Corporation.

The following year, M & D presented a Bill to wind up Hastings Tramways, an obvious prelude to the finish of trolleys. There was public opposition in Hastings, but the council finally agreed by just one vote not to resist the plan. A full takeover came into operation in 1957. Again, initial changes were minor, the quaint 'Hastings Tramways' legend vanishing from the vehicle sides, and 'Town Service' appearing over the numbers of the routes, which had been simplified down from 12 to four basic services. The only postwar extension of wiring was a few yards installed at Hollington so that trolleys could reach a turning circle rather than negotiate an awkward reverser.

Being an isolated system, with a basic fleet size of about 50, there was almost a family atmosphere. Much of the overhead fittings were made and renovated in the well-equipped Silverhill depot. A master of overhead devices, F. J. Cunuder, who was prominent at the Cardiff system later, began his career at Hastings. The town is exposed to the elements and the prevailing south west wind cut carbon collectors' lives to a few hours by salt corrosion. which also wrought havoc with vehicle panels. The system had its quirks: the wires for example, being only 18 in apart instead of the usual 2 ft. The network covered a fairly extensive 22 miles, with gradients as steep as 1 in 9.

Pride of the Hastings fleet was Happy Harold, one of the original 1928 open-top Guys. In the early fifties, members of a transport enthusiasts' society spotted the vehicle, no. 3A, lying derelict in Bulverhythe depot. They suggested it had trourist potential and it was 'done up' in time for the Coronation in 1953 Thereafter, complete with King Harold of 1066 fame as a figurehead, it was a star attraction on the seafront between St Leonards and Fishmarket. Trolley services ended on 31 May 1959. The next day, a civic party made a ceremonial last run from Bexhill to Hastings before lunching at the plush Queen's Hotel. A modern Sunbeam was used—as well as 3A, which still had a future. The booms were fastened down, and a flat and compact Rootes two-stroke diesel engine fitted. Two big 55-amp dynamos and two sets of 24-volt batteries powered the 500 decorative bulbs, which had been no problem when Harold was on the overhead! 'BORN 1928 AND STILL GOING STRONG' ran the slogan on the sides. The vehicle survived a slight fire in May 1965, but was out of service by the early 1970s.

MAIDSTONE

Apart from London's Bexleyheath-based pair of routes, Maidstone developed the only other Kent system, opening a month after Hastings on 1 May 1928. After obtaining the necessary powers in 1923, it was decided to convert the Barming route and inaugurate a new service along Sutton Road to the borough boundary. The first fleet consisted of seven Ransomes double-deckers at £2,005 each, supplemented in 1930 by seven English Electric trolleybuses. Before the first trolleys had run, enthusiasm was clearly not wholehearted, but this had so changed by 1938 that the general manager recommended the small bus fleet be replaced entirely by trolleybuses. As a first phase, ½ mile of extra wiring was erected from the Fountain, Barming, to a new terminus at the Bull. But the war intervened to kill the 'all trolleys' idea.

Maidstone was sited temptingly on the route in and out of London for German bombers, and the trolleybuses were involved in the first raid on the town. The central area was blocked by rubble at the end of October 1940, and an emergency set of wires was strung up around side streets. A national policy of dispersing public transport vehicles also meant that a third stretch of overhead was installed on the town side of the Fountain at Barming to act as an over-night siding for a few vehicles. During the war, Maidstone faced the same small choice of new trolleys as everyone else, and as a result, five utility-bodied Sunbeams were bought in 1943 and 1944. Ten more Sunbeams were added in 1946-7. A period of extreme financial difficulties ensued, plans to buy more new Sunbeams with Northern Coachbuilders bodies being shelved, although trolleys managed to show a £1,185 profit in 1948. The previous year, it had been agreed to provide a service for the new Shepway housing estate, but the existing Sutton Road route was not extended to the fringe of the estate until November 1951 because of financial problems. The route edged along after that: another 180 yd to Nottingham Avenue were added in June 1954, and an extension was opened to the new Parkwood Estate in mid-1959. To work the services, vehicles ran one basic route: from Barming (Bull) to Parkwood, back to Barming (Fountain), off to another spur and terminus at Loose, and then a final trip to the Bull.

Only 32 vehicles were used in all in Maidstone, and to maintain the fleet, the town entered the secondhand market. Three Karrier Ws were acquired when the Llanelly network closed at the end of 1952. They were never successful, entering service in 1955 and being withdrawn five years later. Two Sunbeam Ws were purchased when Hastings ceased trolley operation in 1959, and two BUTs were bought when Brighton closed the same year. Maidstone's depot was in Tonbridge Road, supplemented in later years largely for storage purposes by the former tram shed at Loose. The system was altogether a small-scale affair, and the running of secondhand vehicles brought increasing problems as other operators closed and sources of spares dried up. Post war, relations were often strained with the big Maidstone & District company. Talks on co-ordination of services, a seemingly sensible move, almost succeeded in 1951. In fact, co-operation was 20 years away, but its coming helped doom the golden ochre and cream trolleys. The decision to abandon came in early 1964. The fleet was in a groggy mechanical state by the last day, 15 April 1967. No. 72, one of the Sunbeams bought new, was well decorated and crowded with guests. Looks were deceptive, though, for it had broken down two days before and ran in the final procession with a motor from 64, another Sunbeam. One of the Brighton BUTs, no. 52, failed on the last day itself. Rubbing salt in the wound, the last 24 trolleybuses were replaced by 16 buses sporting a new bright blue livery.

BOURNEMOUTH

This genteel and popular resort wanted to adopt trolleybuses before World War I, and powers were applied for in 1913. As in so many cases, hostilities intervened, and nothing more was heard of the idea until the 1922 demonstration of a Trackless Cars Ltd double-decker to coincide with the Tramways and Light Railways Congress in Bournemouth. The town had to wait another 11 years for its first trolley service, an experimental route from the Square to Westbourne, soon extended from the central terminus to Ashley Road. Four vehicles were ordered initially, including a unique single-deck Thornycroft painted blue, which passed on to South Shields during World War II. There were two AECs, which had dummy radiators and looked like motor buses— they almost deserved the fate of being converted within three years to actual petrol buses. The last of the £7,345 quartet was a Sunbeam with BTH equipment, a type which became the backbone of the fleet. The first batch to be bought consisted of 102 vehicles, the largest single order so far placed.

As routes snaked out through the area, difficulty was encountered in the eastward suburb of Christchurch, where terminus turning space was not available. So the Corporation spent £380 on a turntable installed in a former hotel stable yard and operational from mid-1936. Access was controlled by an indicator light illuminated when the turntable, always an item of great interest, was occupied. It provided reliable service although it had to be closed for six days in May 1958, for overhaul. On the way to Christchurch was another unusual feature, the narrow Tuckton Bridge. Special Ministry of Transport restrictions applied to trolleys using it. The maximum speed allowed was 10 mph, and warning signs announced: 'Trolleybuses must not pass on the bridge.' Until 1942, an extra ½d was added to Tuckton Bridge fares to cover a toll charge.

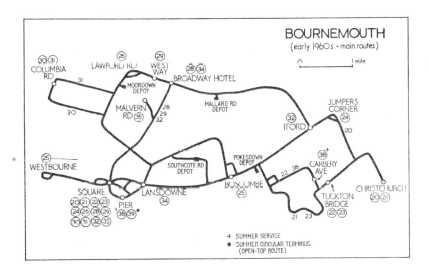

During the 1939-45 war, 30 trolleybuses were despatched from the deserted town to hard-pressed areas, including London, Wolverhampton, Walsall, and Newcastle. The second major batch of trolleys ordered were 24 postwar BUTs, similar in design to the familiar Sunbeams, although the first vehicles to have an all-over primrose livery. The whole fleet followed suit from 1955, lined out first with maroon bands and from 1962 with green. A treat for holidaymakers came in 1958 when three of the original Sunbeams, nos. 200-2, were made open-toppers, a distinction then shared only with Hastings 3A. The seating was increased to 69, and the trio put on a summer circular service.

As far as depots were concerned, there were three originally, at Southcote Road, Moordown, and small premises at Pokesdown. Moordown shut when the corporation opened in 1953 an ultra-modern headquarters at Mallard Road among quiet residential streets in the north of the town. The new depot cost £500,000 and provided column-free covered space for 99 vehicles. The site boasted the largest unsupported span of pre-stressed concrete then in use in the country. Southcote Road closed in 1965, and Pokesdown two years later.

By the late fifties, many authorities had already ditched the trolleybus or were deciding to. But Bournemouth was more than usually concerned with profitable, quiet and clean transport—even though removing the carbon black which tended to smudge the gay primrose paint on the roof and down the back of each trolley was a constant headache—and so the town decided to renew its fleet between 1958 and 1963. Faithful Sunbeams were chosen again, and in the first two years, 30 MF2Bs arrived. The chassis were designed for transit trolleys overseas, and apart from the specifications already noted in Chapter Two, were equipped with rubber bumpers and anti-roll devices. In the last batch, ten were ordered. One was destroyed in a fire at Weymann's Addlestone works, eventually closed in the late sixties, and the other nine arrived in 1962. Last into service, although not bearing the final number in the series, was 301 on 1 November. The last couple of vehicles and one other in Belfast were the only trolleybuses to bear 'reversed' number plates.

Bournemouth was a popular and convenient system for running preserved vehicles as trolleybus services everywhere began to dwindle. Specials were mostly allowed on the streets on Sundays, the corporation charging the enthusiasts either on a mileage basis or by reference to metred electricity consumed. Like Hastings, staff pride was evident. David Chalk, assistant traffic superintendent, would spend Monday to Friday in his Mallard Road office, then on Saturdays turn relief driver, usually with a favourite trolley. The steepest grade on the network was Richmond Hill, 8 mph coasting brakes being fitted to deal with the 1 in 8 descent. Bournemouth had several complicated wiring layouts, one, Winton junction, earning itself the nickname 'the Birdcage.'

Complete with Britain's most up-to-date fleet, Bournemouth planned to go on with trolleybuses until 1973. But the enormous number of cars forced road alterations to which trolleys could not be adapted. The first routes to go were along Lansdowne and St Paul's Roads, resulting in the withdrawal of the open-toppers. In the last few years, bus usage began to drop, and the frequency on a few trolleybus routes dropped to hourly, wholly uneconomic for vehicles geared to intensive service. In some areas, wiring remained after route closures for emergencies, particularly that running to the Pier.

The system, the last on the south coast, eventually finished on 19 April 1969. Included in the final procession was open-topper 202, now preserved. The famous turntable, which had stood on land leased from a brewery, went out of use by buses in 1973 to make way for a hotel extension. Three years after the shutdown, reminders of the trolleybuses still abounded in Mallard Road depot, where vehicles being purchased by enthusiasts were stored, among them 301. Some corporation officials were reportedly surprised when on delivery the final batch of trolleys looked less modern than contemporary motor buses. Sitting alongside replacement Atlanteans, even 301 was basically old-fashioned.

Bournemouth's trolleybus carryings reach a peak as car-less holidaymakers 'invaded' the seaside towns after the war:

	No. of vehicles	Passengers	Receipts
1937	104	26,324,803	£165,506
1947	103	42,735,741	£323,844
1957	103	29,086,555	£427,317
1967	29	11,456,601	£308,268

PORTSMOUTH

A rare combination of environments were served by trolleys in this city of naval establishments, industry, and holiday hotels. Trolleybuses are chiefly remembered for the ferocious battle fought by local residents' associations to prevent abandonment, bitterness being created which must have taken a long time to subside. The first route had been opened on 4 August 1934, running the length of Portsea Island from South Parade Pier via Fawcett Road to Cosham on the mainland. Practice established elsewhere was adopted with 15 vehicles of varying types being tried for experience, including AECs, Leylands, Sunbeams and Karriers. The corporation settled on the AEC chassis design with Craven bodywork, 85 being delivered in 1935 and 1936. The network was put together quickly, just as well for the war affected Portsmouth more immediately than practically any other district in Britain. On the day war was declared three new trolley services, unnumbered, were inaugurated to replace motor buses needed to evacuate children. As the war progressed, Portsmouth's population dropped by a third, and in 1940 routes were diverted away from the seafront area, services being cut from the South Parade and Clarence Piers. The resulting fall in demand allowed four trolleys to be loaned to Pontypridd from 1942 to 1946. Despite heavy bombing, which seriously disrupted rail lines and destroyed ten buses, no trolleybuses were lost, and general manager Ben Hall declared: 'Trolleybuses are best.' One of the enthusiastic trolley operators, Mr Hall designed spark shields to prevent enemy aircraft spotting trolleybus arcing at night, and the design was adopted by many undertakings. The inventive Mr Hall could not prevent the incident of 10 January 1941, when a direct hit on a power station marooned trolleybuses all over the city.

One result of the war was the appointment of women trolleybus drivers, of whom Mr Hall wrote in *Bus and Coach* in June 1944: 'It has not necessarily been found an advantage for applicants to possess more than average physical

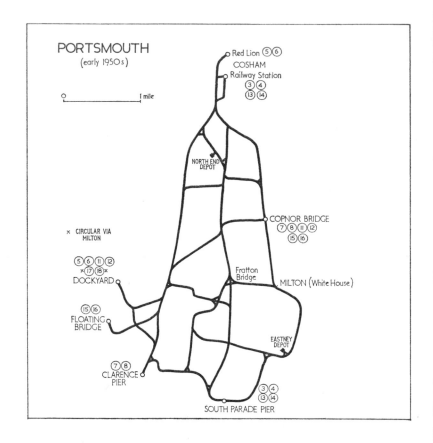

strength.' He thought women 'possessed that light touch which makes for good manipulation of the power controls and rheostatic braking.' First to qualify was Mrs K. E. Devine in October 1941. Six years later, seven female drivers were still at work.

When the war was over, Portsmouth Corporation concluded an early co-ordination agreement with the local company-owned system, Southdown, a move supported by seven per cent of the city's electorate who bothered to vote. In the lean late forties, the maximum use was made of trolleys because of the need for oil economies. Within the city's boundaries, the 21 miles of trolleybus routes carried numbers, while bus services were classified by letters. A popular occasion was the annual decoration of a trolleybus normally to publicise local events. This began when three vehicles were illuminated for the 1935 Silver Jubilee. In 1937, no. 4 was illuminated for the fleet review celebrations; in May 1945, no. 204 was illuminated for the Lord Mayor's Royal and Merchant Navies appeal; the same vehicle was used in June 1950 for an industrial and civic exhibition, turning out again the next year for the industries exhibition at Southsea.

Re-equipment of the fleet—the trolleybus one, this time!—became necessary, and £69,765 was voted towards purchase after an acrimonious debate in the council chamber. At the turn of 1950-1, 15 new BUTs arrived, with Burlingham bodies and English Electric equipment. As far as route extensions were concerned, it had already been decided to restrict trolleys to Portsea Island. The undercurrent of criticism at expenditure on new vehicles followed ironically on a record year for the undertaking, in which trolleys did well. A record surplus of £73,517 was recorded in 1947-8, £13,410 up on the previous 12 months. Trolleys had contributed the lion's share at £53,860. The number of passengers had gone up by four million to 85 million.

Earlier, there had been some unusual praise for trolley crews. On Fratton Bridge (see accompanying map) a multiplicity of routes converged at an extremely awkward junction. 'If we hadn't the best trolleybus drivers in the country I am sure that more than one fatal accident would have taken place at that death trap,' declared a local magistrate at a 1947 election meeting.

The shadows began lengthening in 1955. Although there had been an interesting development that year when a Walsall trolley with a revolutionary Willowbrook body had been seen on three routes for the benefit of a Municipal Passenger Transport Association conference, suspicious residents noticed buses replacing trolleybuses on certain emergency occasions. Rumours of trolleybus withdrawal were at first denied in early 1956 by the chairman of the city's passenger transport committee, but he commented that trolleys were 'obsole-

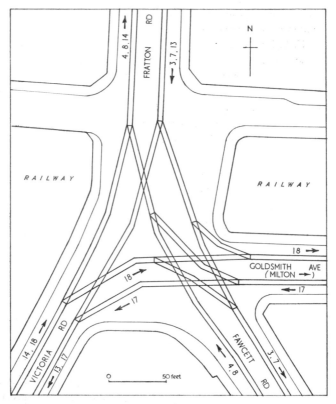

Wiring layout on Fratton Bridge, Portsmouth

scent' and the worst was feared. The decision was not long delayed: in the face of a storm of opposition in the local Press and from ratepayers' groups in Portsmouth and Cosham, the transport committee on 30 July 1956, recommended that gradual withdrawal should begin. In fact one route had already gone, when the original service 1 and 2 from Cosham (Red Lion) to the Dockyard had been replaced by buses M and N. The 1956 decision, together with plans for one-man buses, drew such fire that a firm of management consultants was brought in for an unbiased opinion. One alderman thundered at the critics: 'History will teach us all that the vehicle with maximum mobility must be the machine of the future.' The row continued until the closure of 13 and 14 route to Cosham station in January, 1959. The end came on 27 July 1963. The transport committee had decided on no ceremony, but as

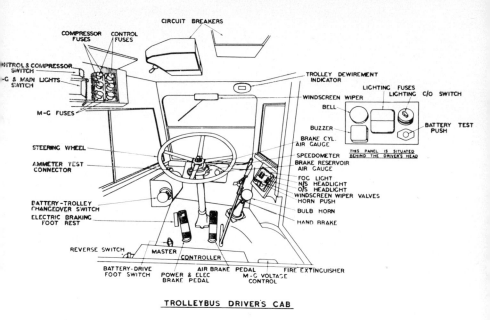

TROLLEYBUS DRIVER'S CAB

Page 89. (*above*) Layout of a typical driving cab. (*below*) Belfast's seven prototypes prepare for service

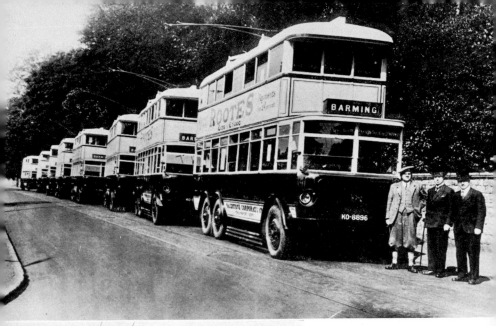

Page 90. Southern scenes. (*above*) Maidstone's first fleet and (*left*) Portsmouth's first vehicle, an AEC of 1934

usual, enthusiasts turned out to mourn. The last regular route was 5/6, although late night runs on the 17/18 were still trolley-worked. The final trolley into Eastney depot, no. 313, was eventually adorned with a wreath of roses by traffic manager A.W. Fielder. Many Portsmouth vehicles ended their days off Portsea Island in a chalk pit at Bedhampton; strangely, anyone following the coast road eastward would eventually reach Southerham, near Lewes, where several of Brighton's trolleybuses finished up in another pit after that town's abandonment two years earlier.

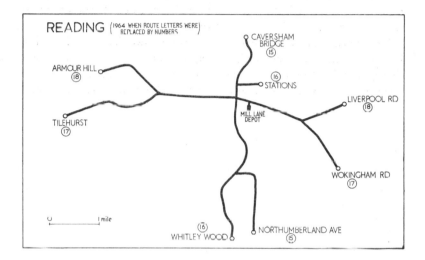

READING

Another town with early ambitions, Reading had powers granted in 1912 after a sub-committee of the tramways committee proposed five possible trackless routes. War and the eventual slump delayed the plans, and it was not until early 1936 that overhead wires were erected to Erleigh Road for trolley-bus driver training. Five vehicles from the leading manufacturers were tried for the Caversham-Whitley route which was formally opened on 18 July 1936 The isolated Erleigh Road stretch, where members of the public were given free rides to accustom them to the new vehicles, remained in position disused for another 19 years. Early trolleys had to be low height because of a restricted bridge on the Caversham route. The problem was got round later by slewing the wires over the pavement and restricting trolleybuses to 5 mph.

H.B.T.B.—F

The Three Tuns to Tilehurst route having been added in 1938, Reading purchased 25 new normal-height AECs with Park Royal bodies and English Electric motors in 1939, the year the last trams ran. Half a dozen utility vehicles ordered during the war ran, unusually, in full corporation livery. Route extensions continued during and after the war, and this necessitated the ordering of 20 new 56-seat BUTs in 1949. These vehicles were 8 ft wide and delivered with air-operated platform doors. A dozen three-axle Sunbeams followed in 1951. The new trolleybuses could not meet the whole need, however, and in 1948 the corporation had purchased a dozen secondhand Karriers at £400 apiece. Like similar vehicles delivered to Maidstone, these Karriers were far from satisfactory, only six actually entering service.

Reading's depot in Mill Lane soon became overcrowded, and at a time when building materials were still hard, and expensive, to come by, a solution was found which had been used with success in Belfast in 1950. A disused hangar was obtained from an airfield near Cambridge and re-erected in Bennet Road, Whitley. It was only operational for eight years because of reductions in the total fleet strength.

Despite that, 12 new Sunbeam F4As with Burlingham bodies were purchased in 1961 complete with flourescent lighting. Reading trolleybuses contributed to an important piece of traffic development. When a section of the main A4 road through the town became one-way, trolleys were allowed to travel on a reserved part of the road against the flow, the first use in Britain of a 'bus only lane', thereafter to be a common method of handling public service vehicles in congested areas. Extensions continued until the last in January 1963, when the Northumberland Road route became 400 yd longer with the addition of wiring to the junction of Whitley Wood Road. Optimism abounded and the chairman of Reading's transport committee was quoted in one of those phrases that ring with a dull thud afterwards: 'Although the town is one of the few still operating trolleybuses, they are here to stay. They are healthier, smoother, quieter—and above all, cheaper.'

There had already been contraction, with the closure of the lightly-used northern end of the Caversham Bridge service on 10 July 1965. In mid-1966, the difficulty of obtaining overhead fittings influenced the decision to abandon altogether, a move which came while the possibility of bridging the 200 yd gap between the south ends of the 15 and 16 routes in Whitley Wood was still under consideration. The 16 closed in January 1967, and the 15 the following Christmas. Route 18 went in March 1968, and the 17 the last, in November 1968. The closure was notable for the remarkable 'farewell' efforts of the local Reading Transport Society. Having intelligently but unavailingly opposed closure, they designed and financed the printing of side advertisements for the last trolleybuses. Local firms were invited at £1 a time (to cover printing costs) to put their name to the banners reading '. . . SAY GOODBYE TO READING'S TROLLEYBUSES.' The final trolleys ran on the 3rd.

Except, it is presumed, to the enthusiast trolleybuses have limited romantic appeal, yet two were used in Reading for wedding parties. On 4 December 1943, no. 102 carried some guests to the Caversham Bridge Hotel, probably because of fuel restrictions. In September 1964, no. 157 was decorated with 'Just Married' front and back for the wedding of the chairman of the Reading Transport Society.

Business on Reading's trolleys mirrored the rest of the country by 'peaking out' in the early fifties:

	Passengers	Revenue
		£
1937–8	2,091,675	9,097
1944–5	24,608,854	141,064
1949–50	26,864,102	202,403
1959–60	19,134,636	310,479
1967–8	11,493,355	252,259

BRIGHTON

Apart from having their redundant vehicles dumped in similar chalk pits, Brighton and Portsmouth shared something else: Brighton's decision to opt for trolleybuses just before World War II was influenced by the exhibition there of one of Portsmouth's AECs in 1935. There was much acrimonious debate in Brighton about trolley proposals, and the whole issue was complicated by the fact that many town services were operated by Brighton, Hove and District, a Thomas Tilling company. As well as Portsmouth no. 20, London Transport's no. 61, the modern member of the former LUT fleet, also made a few trips to help persuade residents to vote for trolleybuses in a town poll. Defeat came at the hands of a House of Lords committee, which was unhappy at that part of the plans dealing with co-ordination with the company system. The problem was resolved in 1938 when new proposals were presented allowing Brighton, Hove and District up to 20 per cent of the trolleybus mileage.

Services finally began on 1 May 1939, when the former C tram route between the Aquarium and Lewes Road became trolley route 48, passing the trolleybus depot in Lewes Road itself. The same day, trolleybuses began on the 26 to Ditchling Road, the former D tram service. Ironically, the trams' disappearance coincided with the retirement as manager of William Marsh, who had supervised the trials of the first Brighton trolleybus in 1913–14. Full-scale services in 1939 were begun by corporation vehicles, 44 two-axle AECs with motors made by the local electrical business of Allen West, which supplied equipment to the whole of Brighton's fleet. Brighton, Hove and District's fleet, also AECs, was not delivered until the war started, and did not enter service until it had ended. They were numbered 6340–7, well distinguished from the corporation's 1–44. Another eight corporation trolleys followed after the war, similar to the earlier ones but made by AEC's successor, BUT, the last of which entered service in 1950. Numbering of these duly carried on to 52. Four other BUTs were delivered for the company, becoming 6391–3. All BH and D vehicles lost the initial '6' digit by the late fifties.

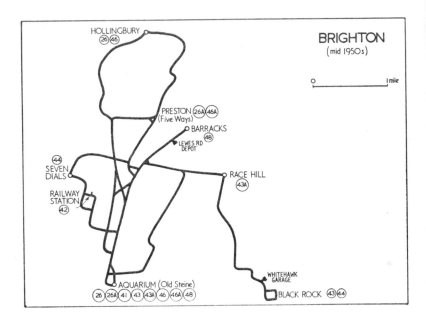

The compact system reached a maximum of 14½ miles, with postwar extensions to Black Rock, Carden Avenue, and eventually, in 1951, to Hollingbury to provide a circular service for the new residential area sprouting on the fringe of the downs behind the town. To a couple of generations of holiday-makers, Brighton's trolleybuses were a familiar sight using the terminus at Old

Steine gardens within sight of the Palace Pier head and the sea. Only 17 years after the introduction of trolleybuses, abandonment was being discussed. Both corporation and company services were subject to some competition from the Southdown company. Co-ordination was the obvious answer, and though talks began, it took over ten years for them to bear fruit. In 1957 and 1958, ten trolleybuses made the fateful journey to the Lewes chalk pit. The first, no. 7, seemed reluctant to leave, becoming wedged under a railway bridge in the Lewes Road while being towed away. The rest of the Lewes-bound batch had to go via Newhaven. In March 1959, trolleybus mileage was cut by half. The last day was 30 June 1961, with final runs to Hollingbury and Preston Drove. A procession was formed, all of corporation trolleys. No. 36, the last vehicle in service, led the way, followed by privately-hired 34, and finally no. 1, full of civic dignitaries. Because of the comparative 'youth' of Brighton's trolleybuses, ten were sold to other operators. Seven corporation trolleys went to Bournemouth, Bradford, and Maidstone, while three company vehicles found new homes in Bournemouth too.

*   *   *

Following World War I, several other undertakings considered trolleybuses but never got as far as inaugurating routes. Tests were carried out for two days in Dover in 1922 with a Railless car which had been built for Ramsbottom. Using a single boom and trailing skate in the tram lines, the vehicle gave demonstration runs on 6 and 7 July to a number of officials from systems who wanted to study trolleys. The venture was declared a success, and Dover's manager, E. H. Bond, was reported to be in favour of trolleybuses to replace his trams as track became due for renewal. Trolleybuses made little headway in the South West, but there were some quiet trials in Bristol. Doncaster Corporation, which had bought motorbuses from Bristol Tramways & Carriage, prevailed on the company to build a trolleybus chassis, and this became the E101, exhibited at the Commercial Motor Show of 1929. Then came E102, designed like the prototype as a high capacity six-wheeler. When a body was fitted, this trolleybus bore a Bristol registration plate. Trials were held in the company's Brislington depot yard, where a negative wire was strung up beside tram overhead. It is thought the vehicle also sallied on to Bristol's streets for a few after-dark trips using a trailing skate for current return. The full-fronted cab projected from the front of the trolley, which also sported protruding headlamps. It became no. 9 in Pontypridd's fleet and was in use from 1932 to 1947. Further west, Torquay Corporation, after approaches from H. T. Barnett, chairman of Torquay Tramways Co, acquiesced in a Bill to install trolleybus traction, but the Devon town saw no further moves. Almost over the border into Cornwall, trolley operation was also studied before the last war by Plymouth.

Before leaving the southern portion of Britain, mention must be made of one wellknown trolleybus owner, the Borough of Epsom and Ewell. This authority bought six vehicles from Huddersfield in 1951, five being converted to mobile conveniences for race meetings on Epsom Downs, the other used for spares. They were in use on 15 Derby days, painted in the council's livery of cream with green lining. All five were handed on to enthusiasts for restoration following their withdrawal in 1970. One of Bournemouth's original fleet of four trolleys which had been converted to a motor bus was eventually sold to Southend Corporation and turned into a ladies' convenience.

CHAPTER FIVE

MIDLANDS AND WALES

MOVING into the heart of England and across to busy, grimy towns in South Wales is to encounter trolleybus services set up for industrial populations. Development was ahead of the South East, two systems having opened in 1914, one of them, Rhondda, dying so quickly that further mention is unnecessary.

ABERDARE

This SouthWales town, described in contemporary technical Press accounts as a 'hive of industry' with a population of 50,000, had opened its network in January 1914, as already noted. The original philosophy was for the Cedes-Stoll trolleybuses to be a stopgap measure until the volume of traffic reached proportions justifying new tram routes. Then the trackless equipment would move further out, and, presumably, the process be repeated. In the event, World War I wrecked the high hopes, which had been hailed as a far-sighted piece of public transport policy. Obtaining spares became wellnigh impossible; there was a particular shortage of armatures which broke frequently. Aberdare's trackless trolleys suffered from the other classic bogey, poor roads, the heavy vehicles breaking up the already dessicated surface. They hung on surprisingly until July 1925, when the prewar schemes were forgotten and ordinary motor buses substituted for the battered trolleybuses. The town's link with trolleybuses was not over, however, for in 1943, Cardiff purchased 43 of Aberdare's traction poles to equip new extensions.

BIRMINGHAM

It is remarkable that Britain's major cities were mostly dilatory in deciding on trolleybus installation. Even though Birmingham was an exception, its early enthusiasm soon faded, and only two basic routes were equipped, without physical connection between them. The general manager who guided the scheme through was Alfred Baker, one of the pre-1914 'pilgrims' who had inspected the early Cedes system in Vienna. Birmingham opened its route to Nechells in November 1922, managing to score a number of firsts in the process. It was the first example of a tram-to-trolley conversion, the first route in the country to be operated wholly by double-deckers, which were in turn the first enclosed vehicles of that type. The early trolleybuses were all fairly bulky affairs, looking much like the solidly-constructed motor buses of the same period. First came a dozen Railless with Roe bodywork, 51-seaters and a full 16 ft high. In 1924, a most interesting vehicle arrived—the chassis was by EMB Ltd, a tramcar equipment manufacturer, and the body by English Electric. It was of lower height construction, and, apart from the solid tyres, considered to be technically advanced. It was not to form part of the fleet for long, being prematurely withdrawn in favour of another order of Railless trolleys which arrived, however, from AEC with bodies by Short Brothers, which had bought up Railless. Four of these vehicles were delivered in 1926. A fifth AEC followed with bodywork by Vickers. All this series, numbered 14-17, still had that stocky bus-look, with projecting cabs and outside stairs, but longer bodies helped relieve the early top-heavy appearance.

No. 18 was a Guy which, by using positive tram wires and a trailing skate for negative return, arrived in Birmingham after travelling from the Wolverhampton factory under its own power. Nos. 19 and 20 had Guy chassis, body and equipment and were demonstrators only used for a couple of months. A third demonstrator, provided by Leyland, was also given the number 19. By this time, the original batch needed replacing, and so 11 new Leylands with GEC equipment were bought. Like Leyland 19, they had half cabs and dummy radiators. The bamboo poles used for hauling down the booms were carried above the saloon windows on the nearside, an uncommon practice found also at South Shields in later years.

In January 1934, Birmingham inaugurated its second route, out along the Coventry Road as far as Yardley (Swan Hotel). It was 5¼ miles in length, and to operate the service, 50 new trolleys were bought from Leyland with motors provided by GEC, and numbered 17 to 66. The previous batch of half-cab Leylands plus five more AECs with English Electric motors delivered in 1932 had taken over the early numbers first used by the Railless trolleys and the various demonstrators. Despite their modern styling, the new Leylands and the AECs retained the city's small destination boxes, with route description and number squeezed into a strip only a few inches deep.

The Coventry Road scheme was extended to a terminus known as 'Coventry Road City Boundary,' which was, in fact, ⅜ mile short of the actual boundary at the Arden Oak Road junction. Services began in July 1936.

With the coming of World War II, Birmingham was a prime target. As nighttime bombing became a real threat, the original Nechells route had to be axed. The reason was two-fold: to get from the overhead in the north west of the city to the depot at Washwood Heath, the trolleys had to use one boom plus a skate in the tram lines. In the blackout, navigating the vehicles along the tracks was extremely difficult, and the flashes from the skate could be seen from the air. So the Nechells trolleybuses were replaced by buses after the end of September 1940. Yet the war was to bring 'compensation' for that route reduction. Important to the war effort was the Rover works in Solihull urban district, just over a mile south of the outer end of the Coventry Road route. Fuel for buses was scarce, and the Ministry of Supply asked Birmingham Corporation to extend trolleybuses to the works. So wiring was erected from a junction with Coventry Road in Sheldon, then running 1¼ rural miles over the city boundary to the factory in Lode Lane, which was the destination shown. Services began 13 months after the Nechells abandonment.

There were two city termini for trolleybuses on the Coventry Road, and most services were numbered in the nineties, apart from 56 and 57, which were short workings to Hay Mills. A few minutes walk from the turnrounds in Albert Street and Station Street was Old Square, from where the unconnected wires took the route 7 trolleys to Nechells. Coventry Road trolleybuses were based at a depot shared with trams about a mile out from the centre.

Trolleys' place in the transport fleet was obviously not a strong one, and in June 1949, the city's transport committee decided to concentrate entirely on motor buses. Ironically, the 'new' trolleys died before the last of the trams. The last run was on 30 June 1951, when a civic party was taken by trolleybus from Arthur Street depot into the city centre, and then on a final return journey behind the last service trolleybus.

WOLVERHAMPTON

Eleven months after Birmingham's hesitating move into trolley traction, Wolverhampton opened a system which was to become one of the most extensive in the country, covering 49 miles at its peak. Curiously, though, it never attracted the same degree of interest as, say, its neighbour Walsall, which operated a joint service via Willenhall. Wolverhampton's trolleybus development, like that in Walsall, was dominated by one figure, but unlike the other network, the influence was felt in the early days.

The first trolleys ran on 29 October 1923. They operated an experimental route, replacing the 2¼ mile Wednesfield tram service, which had been single line with passing loops. The trials were a great success, and further expansion doubled in ten years the traffic which had been handled by tramcars:

	Passengers	Miles	Revenue
Trams 1922–3	14,932,860	1,260,095	£105,046
Trolleybuses 1932–3 (approximate figures)	30,000,000	3,370,000	£214,000

The final trams ran in 1928. The general manager, Charles Owen Silvers, was an ardent supporter of the trackless principle, and he gets much of the credit for transforming 'railless cars' into trolleybuses. Embodying this evolution was Wolverhampton no. 33, unveiled in December 1927. It was the first six-wheel double-decker, a joint product of Guy Motors, a local vehicle builder, and W. A. Stevens of Tilling Stevens, who was a pioneer in the use of petrol-electric traction. The new trolley went into service on the Snow Hill-Sedgley service, and achieved the distinction of rating the first colour plate in the influential *Tramway and Railway World* magazine. The roadway under three bridges had to be lowered to allow use of three-axle trolleys.

Not long afterwards, the 1928 Royal Commission on Transport visited Wolverhampton to study traffic conditions in a typical provincial town. The size of the fleet Mr Silvers inaugurated reached over 350 vehicles, most of them Sunbeams and Guys, logical choices as both had plants in the district. Despite the size of the total fleet, which included only one secondhand trolley, the maximum number of vehicles in use was around 170. The blue Walsall trolleybuses which crossed the boundary at Willenhall ran to a central terminus in St James Square, contrasting sharply with the green and yellow Wolverhampton vehicles. Through running and mixing of fleets was common enough among tram operators, but intermingling of different trolley systems was comparatively rare.

An interesting experiment was carried out in 1949, when *Commercial Motor* staged a road test in Wolverhampton of a new Sunbeam trolley design destined for Western Australia. Apart from the chassis and the BTH equipment, there were only driving and observation cabs fitted. 'KEEP CLEAR. TESTING' was displayed at the rear. It had been expected to stage the test on the route out to Bilston, but this was considered too congested, and the 'trolleybus' operated from Bilston to Willenhall instead. A balancing speed of 34 mph was clocked up, and a top speed of 43.2 mph achieved. At the time, automatic acceleration gear was being fitted to an increasing number of trolleys, but such equipment was not installed in this case. The writer reported approvingly there was 'only one occasion when the driver missed the contacts,' otherwise he operated the controls as skilfully as if automatic facilities were in use.

By 1966, the number of services had been reduced to two basic routes: from Bilston Street to Fighting Cocks, and the other to Dudley via Sedgley. The operation of the 8 to Fighting Cocks was particularly impressive at peak times, when trolleybuses followed one another at intervals of only $2\frac{1}{2}$ minutes. The vehicles were based at Cleveland Road depot, where, to enter service, they had to reverse out into the roadway. Ironically, this method, which had been criticised for many years, had to be employed too at Britain's last operational depot in Bradford. The final day for Wolverhampton was 5 March 1967, when an ex-Rotherham Daimler preserved by enthusiasts appeared on the system, making a special run on the remaining Dudley route. The last trolleybus of all, no. 446, arrived at Cleveland Road depot packed with enthusiasts.

NOTTINGHAM

Trolleybuses were first mooted here as far back as 1908, when the corporation's tramways committee discussed the new Continental traction. Nothing concrete happened until 1925, when a batch of ten trolleys was ordered from the Railless group, which at the time was beginning to shed its chassis-making interests. The General Strike intervened to delay delivery, and services did not begin with the vehicles until 10 April 1927, when they started running from King Street to Nottingham Road. They were the first in a new livery of green and white, and two more were due to follow. But the repeat order was not fulfilled, and it turned out those ten double-deckers from Railless, generally primitive trolleys with solid tyres, were the last the firm produced. Two additional trolleybuses were bought from Ransomes. In 1929, Nottingham supplemented the fleet with six more Ransomes and a similar number of English Electric vehicles.

The decade of the thirties began optimistically with a Bill giving details of multiple route proposals which would have given Nottingham the biggest trolleybus system in Britain at the time. The plan was accepted by the House of Commons but rejected in the Lords, where the descendants of old enemies to trolley expansion, the local county council, objected to the scheme, backed by local bus operators. So expansion had to be gradual, and instead of a huge fleet, 25 new Karriers and Ransomes were acquired. The opponents of 1930 found a supporter eight years later when a new manager, James Gunn, expressed his view that trolleybuses should be abandoned altogether.

By 1931, the Notts and Derby company was on the scene, constructing a long interurban route from the Heanor and Ripley direction to the city boundary at Cinderhill, the corporation erecting overhead from Cinderhill into the centre. Notts and Derby trolleybuses began running on 7 January 1932, with services to Cinderhill in peak hours supplemented by corporation trolleys. Despite the rejection of the 1930 proposals, Nottingham grew quietly to the position where four years later, it was briefly the largest network, soon outstripped by the new London Transport's trolleybus programme.

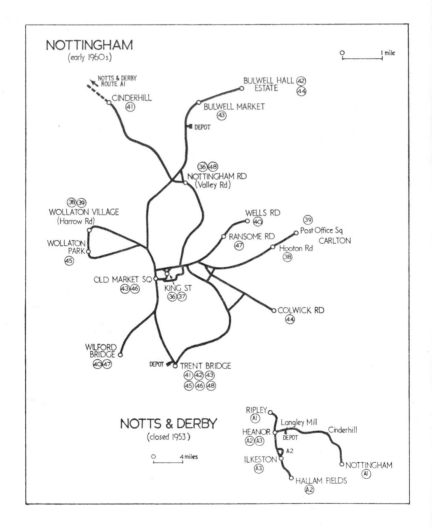

Turning circles or turn-rounds making use of street layouts were always preferred in Nottingham, the only reverser being installed in 1941 at Hooton Road to enable short workings on the Carlton route to turn back to the city centre. Another wartime development was the delivery of half-a-dozen antiquated 'evacuees' from the Hastings network—Guy single-deckers dating from 1928. At the other extreme, the city also received four new 8 ft wide Sunbeams, destined for Johannesburg but diverted because of the war situation. Despite the doubts about trolleys which had been expressed before the war, Nottingham went ahead with building up a modern fleet, epitomised by Roe-bodied Karrier no. 476, the first trolleybus with automatic acceleration, which was purchased in 1945. The following year, the tables were at last turned, with a continental deputation from Lyons in France arriving to study the system, almost 40 years after parties of British engineers and councillors had visited the primitive trolleybus systems of the European mainland.

The last important expansion of Nottingham's fleet came in 1950-2, when the authority put into service 38 BUTs, 25 of them 8 ft wide, plus four new Karriers. The total size of the fleet was almost 300 trolleybuses. Glasgow's revolutionary 'standee' single-decker was tried out in Nottingham in 1953, but it was not popular, passengers being keener to sit than strap-hang.

The possibility of abandonment grew—Notts and Derby having withdrawn in 1953—and the situation was emphasised in 1959, when two councillors asked the transport department to increase frequencies on the city's 'Cinderella' service, the 45 from Trent Bridge to the Wollaton Park beauty spot. Dutifully, the department carried out a survey of the amount of traffic being handled . . . and instead of putting on more trolleybuses, the frequency was reduced! Closure was finally announced in 1962, with routes 38 and 42 becoming partially bus-operated as a prelude to full conversion. The 41, 42, 43 and 46 were replaced by buses early in 1965. The final services, isolated from the depot in Lower Parliament Street, operated until 30 June 1966. The last trolleybus which had been delivered, BUT no. 506, was specially painted and decorated, and the day following closure ran for the benefit of civic representatives and guests.

CHESTERFIELD

Alfred Baker's system at Birmingham had been visited in its second year of operation by a deputation from Chesterfield, which was impressed enough to urge the implementation of trolleybus plans first drawn up in 1912, when the corporation had considered linking the town with destinations which included Clay Cross. At that time, general manager W. G. Marks had reported that trolleys would cost £38,000, some £6,000 more than buses, and indeed motor buses were put on the original trackless routes envisaged.

It was not until May 1923, that trolleybuses appeared on the cross-town route linking Brampton with New Whittington, a distance of five miles. To work it, 14 Straker single-deckers had been ordered the year before. Reeve and Kenning, a local firm, built the bodies, and BTH supplied equipment. Some no-nonsense ratepayers must have been unimpressed with the superstition which persuaded the corporation to number the vehicles from 1 to 12 then 14 and 15. In 1930 rheostatic braking was fitted to the Strakers, which were joined the following year by a pair of BTH-motored Ransomes D2s. Soon, the original Strakers were showing signs of age, and three Karrier-Clough single-deckers were purchased from the defunct York system. The town decided to seek no further replacements, and services finished on 24 March 1938.

PONTYPRIDD

Apart from those short-lived systems like nearby Aberdare which never got beyond the 'trackless' stage, this mining town shared with York the distinction of running the smallest fleet. Yet York only survived a fitful 15 years, whereas Pontypridd went doggedly on with a seven-strong fleet for 27 years, beginning on 3 August 1930. It used mostly Karriers and operated only one route, from Treforest terminus, where vehicles used a reverser, to a colliery at Cilfynydd. On the way, trolleys crossed the River Taff by a bridge on which the overhead was strung up on ornate girder supports.

There were a couple of oddities in the fleet. The Bristol-registered Bristol trolleybus designated E102, which underwent trials in Brislington depot after being built in 1931, went to Pontypridd the following year and was in service until 1947. During World War II, a trolleybus was loaned to the system by Hull. By the time abandonment came along, several of the town's Karriers had already been sold, so, to try and prevent any souvenir hunting, services finished abruptly without notice on 31 January 1957.

WALSALL

As already mentioned in the account of Wolverhampton's system, its neighbour Walsall was fortunate in having a particularly go-ahead influence in its late years, this time in the person of R. Edgley Cox, whom we have already encountered. Having worked with London Transport, during the war with Bradford (where he gained an MSc degree for a thesis on trolleybus acceleration and power consumption) and afterwards at St Helens, he arrived at Walsall in 1952. He proceeded to haggle with the authorities over vehicle size, and pushed through a string of modifications which would have set precedents if trolley-buses had been allowed a long-term future. World War I had prevented the realisation of plans to construct routes from Rushall to Walsall Wood and Bloxwich to Hednesford. In the event, Wolverhampton prompted the start of actual operations by working to its boundary at Willenhall with single-deckers. On 22 July 1931, Walsall's first trolleybuses ran to Willenhall, the initial fleet consisting of four AEC vehicles with English Electric bodies. Wolverhampton was able to put on double-deckers after lowering the road under a bridge at Horsley Fields, and through running began in the November.

From then on, Walsall always purchased Sunbeams, including a quartet of four-wheel utility trolleys in 1943 and 1945. During the war years, the town also borrowed two vehicles from Bournemouth. Until Mr Cox arrived, about the only important change was the livery, the dark blue relief with the basic light blue colour being changed to yellow lining in 1951. The new manager's first move was to get amendments to the legislation affecting Walsall's trolleys, and the Walsall Corporation (Trolley Vehicles) Order Confirmation Act authorised extensions to be built over a ten-year period. This was to cut the expense involved in seeking Parliamentary approval for each new extension or route alteration. In 1953, Mr Cox converted no. 850 (later 350) to pay-as-you-enter, with a seated conductor. There was space for 62 passengers, and 15 could queue for tickets while the vehicle got under way from each stop. The arrangement was not popular, and neither was Glasgow's standee single-decker, used for an experimental period.

The major development came in 1955. While at St Helens, Mr Cox had persuaded the Ministry of Transport Inspectorate to accept a device protecting a low bridge, and the friendly relationship enabled him to negotiate with them to allow trolleybuses of 30 ft in length on two axles. Working closely with Sunbeam, he produced a revolutionary vehicle on the F4A chassis, fitted with a 70-seat Willowbrook body. The vehicle had a somewhat inelegant streamlined shape, and won no prizes for beauty. The Ministry inspectors were intrigued, impressed, and were particularly keen to see whether the new trolley would pass the 25° tilt test. It did, and 15 such vehicles entered service in Walsall in 1955, the same year the first postwar extension, the Blakenhall circular service, was opened. Another seven F4As entered service the next year. Mr Cox's ideas were not limited to vehicle design; the 1954 regulations which permitted the 30-footers also allowed prepayment of fares at St Paul's Street Bus Station, one of the few such termini used by trolleybuses. The prepayment powers were never exercised, but have become particularly popular on the Continent and seem to provide a way round the delays created by one-man bus operation.

A new depot was opened at Birchills in the mid-fifties, and from 1956, the corporation began to purchase secondhand trolleys. Three 1946 vehicles were acquired from Pontypridd, and in 1959, eight ex-Hastings Sunbeam Ws were put on the joint route 29 to Wolverhampton because of their speed capabilities. The F4s which had been operating the service were put on local work. Two Crossleys and four BUTs were picked up from Grimsby-Cleethorpes on closure of that system, and the former Hastings trolleybuses were displaced on the Wolverhampton service in 1962 by eight Sunbeam F4s from the dwindling Ipswich fleet. That same year, hopeful of more Ministry relaxations in size restrictions, Mr Cox prepared a blueprint of a 100-passenger trolleybus, with seated conductor, one entrance, two exists, 32 seats and space for 20 standing downstairs, and 48 seats upstairs. The last extension was in use in early 1963, extra wiring being installed along Bloxwich Lane to Cavendish Road, taking the maximum route mileage to 19.

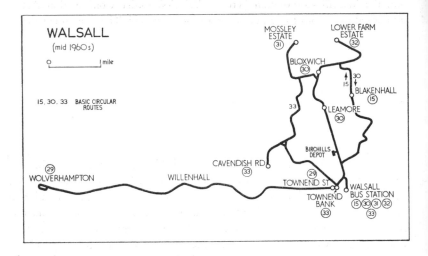

Survival of the trolleybus under strong management looked a safer bet than in most places, but then came a creature of our times which began the decline: a motorway. In this case, it was the M6 pushing northwards between Wolverhampton and Walsall and cutting across the line of the joint route. A new bridge had to be constructed over the M6 to carry the existing roadway, and it was proposed to install special ducts for the necessary trolley cabling. The main objection, however, was the remote yet dangerous possibility that accident or

Page 107. (*above*) Relatively plush interior of 1938. (*below*) Notts and Derby's Hallam Fields terminus a month before the 1953 closure

Page 108. (*above*) Three of R. Edgley Cox's Walsall Sunbeams loom. (*below*) Through a forest of overhead, a Glasgow trolley on route 105

even high wind could bring the overhead wiring down on to the motorway. So route 29 closed in 1965. Almost certainly, it could have only lasted another two years anyway because of the conversion of Wolverhampton's trolleybuses. Innovation was not dead, though, and the introduction of a new one-way scheme in Walsall to speed traffic gave Mr Cox the chance to lengthen one of the F4s which re-entered service in December 1966.

On 1 October 1969 services in Walsall came under the control of the new West Midlands Passenger Transport Executive, part of the effort to make public transport economic. Mr Cox became chief engineer, and in this role decided to try again with pay-as-you-enter, repeating his 1953 experiment 16 years later with a former Bournemouth Sunbeam MF2B. Tentatively, it was thought this could be the forerunner of 28 new trolleybuses, but the forming of the pte and manufacturers' unwillingness to provide small batches of vehicles sealed the trolleys' fate. Secondhand vehicles were taken off the road and replaced by buses on 16 February 1970, and all services finished on 2 October. The next day, a special procession of four trolleys ran from the central bus station to Bloxwich, and when in the evening the procession turned into the depot, Mr Cox was at the wheel of the final vehicle, a decorated 872.

Afterwards, in a foreword to an enthusiasts' handbook on the Walsall network, he wrote of the 'natural regret I feel under the circumstances of what I regard as closure before proper fulfilment.' Just a week before he finally retired from the pte in Birmingham at the end of 1972, he offered his definition of the many modifications he had introduced. He declined to let them be remembered as 'gadgets.' 'I would prefer,' said Mr Cox, 'to call them improvements.'

NOTTS AND DERBY

The Nottinghamshire and Derbyshire Traction Co operated a trolleybus service that was without exact parallel anywhere in Britain. As mentioned already, it was an interurban system, plunging into the countryside, mostly offering fairly wide intervals between successive trolleybuses. In that respect, the company defied the principle that trolleys were designed to make high-frequency, stop-start runs.

Its network, consisting of three routes operating in a T shape, was based on two separate tram systems, that between Nottingham and Ripley, and another from Heanor south to Hallam Fields, via Ilkeston. The company's blue trolleys covered 16 miles on the principal route, the A1 from Nottingham's King Street and Queen Street city terminus to Ripley, probably the longest trolleybus route in Britain. The A2 and A3 travelled south from Heanor, the point at which the A1 turned north for Ripley. Although Notts and Derby covered 26 miles in all, it managed with a fleet of 30 vehicles. When the system closed after 21 years on 25 April 1953, Notts and Derby's entire fleet of AECs and BUTs was bought by Bradford Corporation. The firm was associated with the Midland General Omnibus Co, and a special Act of Parliament was required to arrange the co-ordination of existing bus services with the replacement Midland General buses.

DERBY

Two days after the Notts and Derby system began life, trolleybuses were inaugurated in Derby itself, although completely unconnected with the company network which shared municipal wires in Nottingham. Derby's first route, on the Nottingham Road, was opened on 9 January 1932, and progressively, services were handed over to trolleybuses between then and 1943, when the last new section of overhead was erected to Sinfin Lane. To start services, a fleet of 13 Guy BTX six-wheelers was purchased, together with the usual batch of guinea pigs being given a chance to prove themselves. In this case, there was a Karrier, a Sunbeam, and a Ransomes vehicle.

As old tram services disappeared, Derby added more BTXs, fitted mostly with Rees Roturbo 75 hp motors. The early vehicles were aptly described as 'piano fronted' with their stepped appearance; the first 'modern' vehicles appeared in 1938 when delivery was taken of two-axle Daimlers.

When war came along, more Guys were added with 1928 Hastings single-deckers being drafted in, part of the same fleet which had been evacuated to other parts of the quieter Midlands. It was not all that quiet, however, with wartime conditions hitting the system in a quite unexpected way on the second day of hostilities. Trolleybuses were marooned when a number of barrage balloons were struck by lightning. Their cables drifted down and fouled trolley overhead, as well as other supply lines, telephone wires, and even railway lines. The first two winters of the war were grim, and Derby's trolleys suffered badly. Apart from icy roads, broken bracket arms on the overhead presented an unusual hazard. Things were so difficult that temporary withdrawal of the trolleybus services was actively considered.

After the war, the Guy name vanished, but Derby continued buying from the same source, taking delivery of 53 Sunbeam F4s between 1949 and 1953. During this period, the first abandonment occurred, with the Chaddesden Park Road route being dropped, cutting the network back from its peak of 27.91 service miles. Nevertheless, purchase of vehicles went on, with a final eight Sunbeam F4As with Roe bodies entering service in 1960. The next year, only

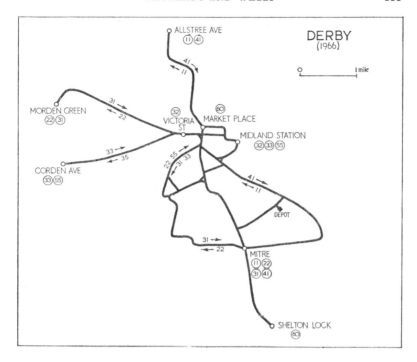

one depot, at Ascot Drive, was used, Nottingham Road and Osmaston Road having lost their trolleys.

When Chaddesden Park Road trolleybuses had been withdrawn, the wiring stayed up for specials, and this was a continuing feature of Derby operation. There were various other curiosities. At the roundabout at Alvaston (Blue Peter), trolleys traversed a section of road banned to other traffic. Vehicles running to the depot or making one of the many short workings, carried numbers like 00, 01, 02 and so forth, more commonly seen as headcodes on multiple-unit electric or diesel trains. Another strange sight noted in the mid-sixties by a pair of watchful observers, R. D. H. Symons and P. R. Creswell, was that of drivers being trained while in charge of service trolleys. L plates were draped front and back, and the wide cab would comfortably accommodate trainee and instructor. Passengers' reaction was not recorded!

Closure came in 1967, which with 1966, shares the distinction of having the most abandonments, four systems being shut down in each year. The last Derby trolleybus ran on 10 September, arriving at the depot quarter of an hour after midnight. The vehicle, no. 236, had been chartered the previous day to take enthusiasts on a tour of most of the available routes.

LLANELLY

Back on South Wales, Llanelly was another small network of no great distinction, apart from the unusual fact that it was owned by an electricity supply concern, Llanelly and District Traction Co. The system was opened on 26 December 1932, closing just over a month short of 20 years later, on 31 November 1952. At the end, 27 vehicles were in use, a number of which were purchased by Bradford and Maidstone. The Kent town probably rued the day it acquired its batch, for the Karriers involved gave indifferent service.

The peculiar ownership of Llanelly and District was responsible for the trolleys' demise. On the nationalisation of the electricity supply industry in the late forties, the fleet became part of the South Wales Electricity Board, making the trolleys unique, directly State-owned vehicles. The board, however, turned them over to South Wales Transport Co, part of British Electric Traction, which decided on abandonment.

CARDIFF

The capital of Wales shared with the principal city of Scotland a tardy approach to trolleybus installation. In the end, Cardiff opened Britain's second to last system, and Glasgow the last, in 1949. Cardiff had less excuse, because the corporation's interest in trolleys went right back to 1911, when the chairman of the tramway committee and the system's manager visited the new Bradford layout and returned enthusiastic about trolleybuses. Shortage of funds in the depressed conditions of the twenties and thirties pushed the subject into the background, and when trolleybuses were discussed again, starting in 1936, there was a remarkable controversy, with figures being bandied about in the council chamber supporting widely divergent conclusions. In the slum district of Temperance Town, the state of the tram track meant that new traction was necessary. The transport committee, with an eye to flexibility, urged buses—but the electricity committee, seeing a promising customer in the wings, was in favour of trolleybuses. An important problem was the restricted height under three bridges and the twin spans at Queen Street, although this difficulty was resolved when the Ministry of Transport agreed to make an exception and allow the clearance between vehicle roof and bridge structure to be lowered from 12 in to 6 in. Now began the battle of statistics. The transport manager calculated that trolleybuses would incur an annual deficit of just under £6,768, compared with an annual profit of nearly £1,908 for buses and a tram deficit of £1,740. He based his figures on running costs of 10.9684d per mile for trolleybuses and 9.7836d for buses. Costs quoted at various contemporary conferences were in basic agreement with the trolley figure, but bus expenses were usually put over 2½d higher. Trolleys were usually given the edge for gross profits. Comparison is always dangerous, but it is instructive that the city treasurer disagreed with his colleague so far that he put the profits of trolleybus operation at over £23,000 and buses at £18,000. By 37 votes to 14, the city council, surely bemused, accepted trolleybuses. In fact, when they got under way, trolleybuses showed a surplus of £266 in the first month of operation, an annual rate of £3,000. The decision to go ahead, taken in March 1939, could not have come at a worse time, of course. A contract was placed with Leyland for chassis, with GEC electrical gear and bodies from Northern Counties, of Wigan. In June 1940, Leyland was switched to war work, and Cardiff's first fleet arrived as AECs. The first route, from Clarence Road to Wood Street, was inaugurated by the Lord Mayor on St David's Day, 1 March 1942.

He had officially opened the 2½ mile service by inserting a penny in a pay-as-you-enter box which allowed Cardiff trolleybus passengers to pay the lowest fares in Britain at the time. The scheme was extended to trams in 1943 and buses the year afterwards; it was found in 1946 that the average distance being travelled for a penny was 2.38 miles, compared with a shade under one mile in 1940. Those trolleys with a front exit to aid pay-as-you-enter operation eventually had it sealed up in 1954, although two staircases remained. Seven 1930 single-deckers were bought from Pontypridd to inaugurate the 16 route in August 1947. These lugubrious vehicles were known as 'Doodlebugs' and struggled along with a top speed of 18 mph. Then the corporation order 70 double-deckers and 5 single-deckers from AEC. Northern Counties could not supply the bodywork, so an arrangement was reached with Bruce Coachworks at Pengam Airport. Trolley 246 emerged from there in October 1949, the first to be bodied on Welsh soil.

Roath depot, reached at first by trolleys using traction batteries until the wiring pushed out to Pengam, was equipped in 1951 with an Essex trolleybus washer, designed to descend through the wiring. About the time Glasgow's standee trolley was making demonstration runs in England, Cardiff equipped single-decker 238 to provide 30 seats and room for 30 standing. The travelling public was still about 15 years away from this form of travel, and 238 was soon reconverted. The last route extension in Wales was opened in mid-1955 when trolleys were laid on from Havelock Street to Ely, on route 10A and 10B. Interestingly enough, the road to Ely had been laid out in the first place with central reservations to allow trams to run on reserved track. Trolleybuses made indirect use of the reservations, the South Wales Electricity Board digging up the grass to lay cables for the trolley supply. Fourteen vehicles replaced 16 buses on the route, and Cardiff's fleet reached its maximum size of 79 trolley-buses.

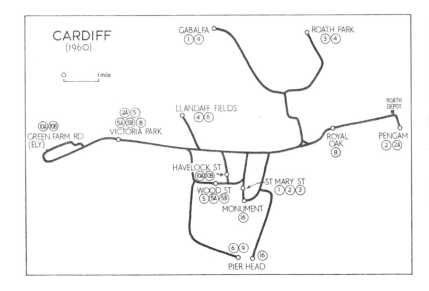

Having started at Hastings, F. J. Cunuder, as deputy general manager and engineer, did some interesting work in Cardiff on overhead gear. He perfected a new trolley head, reducing the carbon insert length from around 92 mm to 64 mm, designed to cut down the 'fore and aft' movement at the top of the trolley boom and so help stop dewirements. Mr Cunuder also developed a new method of frog changing, devising a frog with tongues made of springy copper which would change if the vehicle was driven under the frog itself under power, rather than through a preliminary skate. The point of divergence would be 100 ft from the actual turn-out, and the interlaced wires spaced 4 in apart in the intervening distance.

Decoration of trolleybuses for civic events was popular, beginning with the golden jubilee of the transport undertaking in 1952. Fifty years of city status was the theme for 1955; the Commonwealth and Empire Games in 1958; the National Eisteddfod in 1960; shopping festivals in 1962, 1963 and 1964; and a

Father Christmas parade in 1964, when the leading trolleybus disgraced itself by bursting into flames. Christmas processions were repeated in 1967 and 1968. On the debit side, Cardiff had the doubtful distinction of being the only authority to demolish homes to make way for trolleys: this happened at Gabalfa when a private stretch of road was constructed in May 1961, to provide a new turn-round and two houses were levelled. That same year, when a magic number of sorts had been passed, trolleybuses having made accumulated profits of £100,000 since inception, it was decided to abandon. Services into the city from Pengam went first in November 1962; the famous single-deckers, the last in Britain, were withdrawn from route 14 (re-numbered from 16) on 11 January 1964. The end was complicated by a dispute among the corporation's transport workshop staff, and services on the 10A and 10B to Ely, which had been scheduled to finish on 11 January 1970, were curtailed on the previous 3 December. Tours were run on 9 and 10 January, and special last day runs took place on the 11th. Having been the penultimate starter, Cardiff trolleybuses were followed into extinction by four other systems.

CHAPTER SIX

THE NORTH AND SCOTLAND

TROLLEYBUSES had begun in the North with Leeds and Bradford staging their double openings on 20 June 1911, and the idea took hold quickly. Of the 25 systems described in the area in this chapter, 19 were in operation before trolleys first ran in London. Glasgow, however, remained dominated by trams until it inaugurated Britain's last trolleybus system in 1949.

LEEDS

It has already been noted that Leeds deserves the distinction of the first trolley operator because its services ran continuously from the first day. The original four single-deckers which pioneered the Farnley route from Thirsk Row were supplemented by others of a similar design in 1915 and 1921. On 9 September 1915, a new route was opened from White Cross, Guiseley (opposite the renowned fish and chip restaurant owned by Harry Ramsden) to the town of Otley. The starting point was ten miles north west of the city centre, and the route was sparsely populated. Even so, a spur to Burley-in-Wharfedale was opened on 22 October and a 30-minute headway maintained to that point, compared with 15 minutes on the Otley service. It was an attempt to provide a worthwhile rural facility. Even today, and imagining a small car-owning population, the available traffic would not justify such capital expense on vehicles and roadside equipment, and it was soon found the cars were poorly patronised. Nevertheless the isolated nature of the area allowed some exciting, unofficial running: the stated maximum speed was 12 mph, but 25 mph was often achieved on the downgrade into Otley, where cars terminated at the Maypole. In August 1921, Leeds unveiled car 510, a double-decker. It was a cumbersome vehicle, seating 59 in covered comfort of sorts. The electrical gear was housed in a swivelling forecarriage, carried under the projecting driver's compartment. The revolutionary front wheel drive was powered by two 25 hp motors patented by G. A. Bishop and manufactured under licence from a Leeds firm, Electric Traction Co. The carriage was attached to the main frame by six bolts, the idea being to make it readily detachable in case of failure. Mr Bishop's system was tried without great success in nearby Keighley. The technical Press was particularly impressed by 510's low loading line, the rear platform being only 15 in from the road surface. This was 'an enormous advantage to those passengers who have lost activity and joint flexibility,' observed *Commercial Motor*. 'Many of these passengers are lost to the services which do not cater for them, yet they all constitute potential additional revenue, and they invariably travel during the slacker hours of the day, so that the business is worth aiming at.'

Success with 510 persuaded the corporation to go ahead with 511 and 512, basically similar and designed to replace single-deckers to Farnley. In June 1922, Trackless Cars Ltd produced 513, the high-capacity double-decker already encountered being tried out at Bournemouth and in London United Tramways' area. This 60-seater was built to the order of Trackless by Blackburn Aeroplane and Motor Car Co, another Leeds business. After its demonstrations, 513 entered service in Leeds in February 1924.

As the new double-deckers tackled the Farnley services, 1911-style single-deckers plied the country lanes to Otley and Burley. Intriguingly, powers were granted in 1925 for the overhead to be extended south from Guiseley to Baildon Bridge, then over any available trackless extension into Bradford, a fascinating potential link between the pioneering networks. Independent bus competition killed the plan, however, and in July 1926, the uneconomic trolleybus services based on Guiseley were withdrawn. Through motorbuses from Leeds were put on to cover the routes at first, but these in turn were cut back to Guiseley. A hard look at trolleybus operation had been taken by William Chamberlain, a Lancashire man appointed general manager in early 1926. He turned his attentions to the Farnley trolleys, and the prospect was bleak there too. In early 1928 the city's transport committee reported that trolleybuses were carrying short distance passengers, who, given the chance, would get off and catch the 'more comfortable and more convenient' motor-buses. The end came on 26 July 1928, and Leeds devoted itself to building up a large tram and bus operation.

BRADFORD

This system's blue trolleybus fleet, which totalled almost 260 vehicles over the years, including 85 second and even thirdhand trolleys, was more closely chronicled by enthusiasts than any other. Mostly, this was because it remained an extensive operation right into the sixties, and having shared the honour of being first, Bradford attracted wide interest and publicity by running Britain's final trolleybuses.

Extension of the original Dudley Hill-Laisterdyke route began when trolleys reached Bankfoot on 17 July 1914. Eighteen single-deckers were built by the corporation at Thornbury, the original pair having been renumbered and converted to goods vehicles. No. 502 became a trolley battery vehicle in May 1916, to carry goods and parcels. As well as standby batteries, it was equipped with a single pole and trailing skate. From November 1918, it was making regular parcels trips to Leeds via the joint tram route. In 1920, when the vehicle was making two return journeys a day between Bradford and Leeds, its operating costs were reckoned at between 20 and 25 per cent less than a conventional petrol vehicle.

In 1920, still using its own manufacturing facilities at Thornbury depot, Bradford Corporation built the first covered top double-decker trolleybus, numbered 521. It made use of many tram-type parts, including a 45 hp motor by Dick Kerr. The Ministry of Transport, relaxing weight regulations, made it clear that Bradford's manager, R. H. Wilkinson, took responsibility for any trouble arising from the revolutionary construction. 521 was 15 ft 4 in high and weighed just five tons; among the transport authorities impressed was Birmingham, about to equip its first trolleybus route. Representatives of undertakings from all over the country were in Bradford again two years later to study 522, a 48-seater which was the first to have a foot controller, allowing drivers the luxury of keeping both hands on the steering wheel. It was fitted with a 70 hp Metrovick motor. This rumbling pair of giants went into service on the Bolton-Bankfoot route.

The original concept of trolleybus operation was to use them on thinly-populated routes where trams were not justified. Bolton-Bankfoot was rather too quiet, and from New Year's Day 1923, seven one-man-operated single-deckers were put into operation. The folding door was closed by a driver's lever, which also bolted it and lifted up the lower outside step. These vehicles could carry 30 passengers, and operating costs were reckoned at 4d to 6d per mile less than two-man vehicles. Current collection on this pay-as-you-enter batch was by a soft iron shoe fitted in the trolley head, a method favoured by Mr Wilkinson, but which was found to shorten the life of overhead wire. A more practical device perfected about this time by Mr Wilkinson was a cab indicator to show the driver the position of his vehicle in relation to the overhead. One possible answer to the problem of economic running was the suggestion of an early version of what were to be called standee vehicles—

Bradford considered in the early 1920s a trolleybus with 37 seats and space for 25 standing. The proposal was rejected.

Bradford described its fleet throughout the twenties and thirties as 'Railless Electric Vehicles', although in 1925-6, a new batch of weak-field equipped single-deckers for the Clayton route, numbered 532 to 539, were described as 'trolleybuses.' At this time, Bradford also took delivery of the seven unique Associated Daimler trolleys, the city's first pneumatic-tyred vehicles. The 532-9 vehicles were recalled nearly 50 years later by a retired driver, Arthur Green. 'This type did not last long,' he told me, 'as they were considered dangerous owing to bad steering.' This caused trouble on one occasion when a man was sacked for bad driving 'and only concerted action by the rest of the drivers had him reinstated.' Mr Green started driving in 1926, when solid-tyred vehicles still abounded; as they bumped over the roads paved with setts 'the vibration was terrible.' Of the early trolleys in general he remembered: 'They were slow and not fitted with any wipers. The lamps in front were, I think, 40 watt bulbs. Of course, speed was not needed as the times allowed for each trip were ample.' One hour was allowed for the Bolton-Bankfoot round trips, and half-an-hour on the Bradford-Frizinghall, Bradford-Bolton Woods and Oakenham-Bankfoot runs. Problems constantly arose with dewirements, an equal nuisance on the trams, and Mr Green recounted a story (probably apocryphal!) told of a former Bradford traffic superintendent: 'He had occasion to complain to a certain tram driver that his reports of trolley accidents were too long and verbose. The man, whose name was Gilligan, sent in his next report . . . "Off again, on again, gone again. Gilligan".' Trolleybus crews saw the funny and real side of that tale.

The converted pair of RET cars which had inaugurated services survived until the mid-twenties. Double-deckers 521 and 522 were withdrawn by 1927, the latter ending up as an office store. As replacement of tram routes started under plans laid out in a 1929 Bill, 25 double-deckers were bought from English Electric. They were six-wheelers, never popular in Bradford. Supporting the proposals for widespread use of trolleybuses, the transport department produced some impressive figures for 'miles per failure.' For buses it was only 910, for trams 2,100, and trolleys 3,700. The third batch of 'outside' double-deckers, nos. 597 to 632, were fitted with regenerative as well as rheostatic brake control, and staff recall the times when application of the regeneration equipment caused current surges which blew out the light bulbs in the passenger shelter at Hall Ings in the city centre. An important date was 2 October 1935, when trolleybuses began operating route 8 to Duckworth Lane, extended six months later to the Royal Infirmary. It was the busiest service in Bradford, despite its small mileage, and was destined to be the last service in the country operated intensively by trolleys.

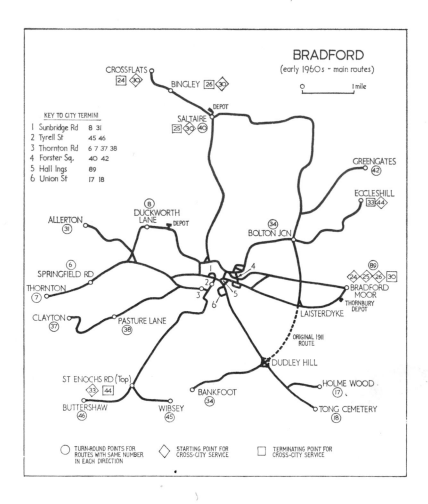

During World War II, four AEC vehicles were hired from Southend, the most modern trolleybuses in that fleet and considered too valuable to operate in a strategically-important coastal area. Ten Sunbeams constructed for Johannesburg were diverted to Bradford, among the many British-built trolleybuses which never reached South Africa. With Bradford during the war was the redoubtable R. Edgley Cox who experimented with carbon inserts, which replaced trolley wheels from mid-1942.

Postwar, a well-liked general manager was Chaceley Humpidge, a vigorous pro-trolleybus official with experience at Birmingham, Portsmouth and Nottingham. Although his policy was to push through more route conversions and extensions, the first signs of retrenchment actually appeared in the late forties with a proposal for route 20 to Undercliffe being dropped. After 1950-1, Bradford embarked on extensive buying of used vehicles, its last new batch being eight BUTs with Weymann bodies. In September 1952, it contracted to purchase the soon-to-be-withdrawn Notts and Derby fleet of AECs and BUTs, moving on to acquire ten of the Llanelly fleet, former Darlington single-deckers rebodied as double-deck, ex-St Helens, Brighton and Hastings vehicles, and six unique third-handers purchased from Doncaster and rebodied in 1962 having been acquired originally from Darlington in 1952. Bradford's last trolleybuses, ex-Mexborough single-deckers rebodied by East Lancashire, entered service in 1963, the last of all, no. 847, on 1 March.

As for services, a 2½ mile route to Wibsey had been equipped in 1955, to the relief of drivers who had asked for trolleybuses because of the arduous gradients encountered. The last extension of all was opened on 6 March 1960, when trolleybuses began using a spur from Tong Street to the Holme Wood housing estate, where trolleys used a reverser in Knowles Lane. In 1961, Bradford remembered the early days and celebrated the golden jubilee of trolley traction, one of only three systems which survived long enough to do so, the others being Rotherham and Teesside. For the occasion, Bradford 603, an AEC of 1934, was painted up in 1911 colours, complete with ornate lining out.

Road alterations began having a crucial effect on trolleybus routes in the early sixties, the City-Bradford Moor and Eccleshill-St Enoch's Road Top services going in November 1962. The actual decision to abandon had been taken the previous year. Trolleybus supporters noted that the storm of criticism which was aroused provoked 75 letters to local newspapers, the biggest postbag on a single subject since the last war. The Crossflatts route ended in 1963, and the 1911 route disappeared after the end of February 1964 when trolleybuses were dropped from Bolton-Bankfoot, although most of the wiring remained in place. So the system declined. The changed conditions were exemplified by the fitting of two-way radios to four trolleybuses after crews had complained of late-night attacks. Almost unbelievably, Bradford trolleys managed the diamond jubilee, with four vehicles, including the latest and oldest available, making special tours of the remaining routes. A major link with the past was broken on 31 July 1971, when Thornbury depot, where many early trolleys had been built by corporation staff, was closed for passenger services. The last two operational services were the 7, the cross-city Thornton-Thornbury route, and the 8 from Sunbridge Road terminus in the city to Duckworth Lane. On 7 November, buses moved into Duckworth Lane depot.

The last of all last days was scheduled for the following March, but suddenly, it looked as though Bradford would be 'robbed' of its trolleybuses prematurely. A national coal strike caused a drastic reduction in power supplies, and this forced suspension of the remaining trolleys on 11 February 1972. In the weeks that followed, consultations were held with the Yorkshire Electricity Board to allow trolleybuses to make the occasional journey across the city from Duckworth Lane to Thornbury for maintenance. Happily, current was restored on 7 March, and for two-and-a-half weeks, Bradford was Mecca for trolleybus enthusiasts. Trolleys were seen mostly on the Duckworth Lane route in peak hours. In the chilly, fading light of late afternoon, enthusiasts would cluster outside Duckworth Lane depot as a handful of trolleybuses were reversed out for evening duties. Eleven were licensed for operation in March. Nineteen others were in store, and there was one learner vehicle, no. 743, fitted with a dual foot brake. Many were the extra passengers as the trolleys swept down into the city via the Toller Lane dual carriageway, performing impressively on the adverse gradient on the return journey, accompanied by the popping of photographers' flash bulbs.

Seats cost £1 each on the special tours run on the penultimate day, Saturday, 25 March. The following day, trolleybus 844 turned out with 'BRADFORD'S LAST TROLLEYBUS' on the front, rear and off-side advertisement panels, and, for good measure, 'BRITAIN'S LAST TROLLEYBUS' on the nearside. A police escort was provided as the vehicle made the farewell trip from Thornton through the city to Thornbury depot. Aboard were civic dignitaries and guests who included Edgar Oughtibridge, then 80, a former maintenance superintendent who had worked on the 1911 cars. When the party reached Thornbury, the power was ceremonially turned off by the Lord Mayor, Ald. Herbert Moran, who declared: 'We shall miss the fume-free silent service of the trackless trolleybus.' The hordes of enthusiasts were a source of concern to the transport department, and I was told later that a secret memo was circulated stating that the police had been asked to 'arrest' any privately-owned trolleybus sneaking on to the system and literally stealing electricity. Preserved vehicles had made guest appearances on other last days, but none were allowed in Bradford.

ROTHERHAM

Development of trolleybuses in Rotherham—which had opened Britain's fourth network in 1912—did not follow the Bradford pattern, as single-deckers remained firmly in favour until an unexpected economic crisis in the fifties led to a batch of vehicles being converted to double-deck.

The trio of early RET vehicles were replaced by single-deckers of much the same sort as operated by the Mexborough and Swinton concern, with which an interlinked route was inaugurated in 1929. The system grew to a size of 12.63 miles, and electric traction was shown off to particular advantage by the town famous also for its single-ended tramcars. In 1941, Rotherham's services boasted the highest schedule speeds for trolleybuses in the country.

The main route was that across the centre of town, linking Kimberworth and Thrybergh, and this service was the last to be extended, when, in 1948, half-a-mile of new wiring was added at the Kimberworth end. Contraction began only the next year however, with the trolleybus service to Templeborough being withdrawn at the same time as the Sheffield tram route. Two more trolley routes were cut in 1951, and three years later the pioneer run between Heringthorpe Lane and Maltby was taken over by buses.

The general manager at the time, Norman Rylance, had to report that trolleys were losing money, and an abandonment programme was pushed ahead. Everything changed in 1955, when Rylance's successor found that financial difficulties made taking on a large loan for new buses impractical. As found elsewhere, trolleybus replacement was being promoted despite the fact that almost new vehicles were in use. No less than 46 single-deck, six-wheel Daimlers with East Lancs bodies had been delivered in 1949-50 at a cost of £250,000. Extra capacity was urgently needed, so the new manager recommended scrapping the abandonment plan and converting a number of the new single-deckers to double-deck. Fourteen were so equipped, the 38-seat bodies being replaced by 70-seat Roe bodies at a cost of £2,300 each. It was an innovative approach to a problem tackled similarly, though with less urgency, in Bradford. Apart from the Daimlers' recent delivery, the Rotherham transport department also argued that the intended expansion of nuclear power plants made electric street traction look attractive. There were, however, those who argued against this that nuclear generating stations were hugely expensive, and worse, less efficient than conventional installations. Caught by rising power charges and non-availability of equipment, Rotherham's trolleybuses 'bought' themselves a ten-year reprieve by conversion to double-deck, the system closing eventually on 2 October 1965.

STOCKPORT

As mentioned earlier, this southern satellite of Manchester plumped uniquely for the Lloyd Kohler or Bremen current collection system when it opened in 1913. The system itself has already been described; it was highly impractical, although similar installations have been successful powering electric vehicles inside factories. Reasonably efficient service was maintained in Stockport with the three Daimler cars, but World War I cut the source of spares, and the network was doomed early. Barely a year after hostilities were over, the single route connecting the town with the village of Offerton shut down officially on 7 October 1919, although occasional trips afterwards were reported.

KEIGHLEY

Bradford's neighbour adopted the Cedes-Stoll collection apparatus, equipping three routes: the original from Ingrow to Cross Roads (opened in 1913) and subsequent services from Keighley to Oakworth and Utley to Eastburn. In 1916, when the familiar bogey of poor roads was beginning to damage equipment, the corporation decided to extend the Cross Roads route to Oxenhope, although the spares shortage and county council opposition delayed the actual opening for five years. In the meantime, Keighley purchased the double-decker which had been tried without success in Hove. The vehicle, first numbered 9 and later 59, entered service in Spring 1917, having been acquired from the Cedes group's British subsidiary, wound up on Government orders because it was the agency of an enemy power. The double-decker was tried out on the Eastburn service, and the feelings of the passengers on the open top deck can only be guessed as the collection trolley—Stanley King, chronicler of the system, reports it was nicknamed the 'blind man's dog'— swished past as the car tackled different gradients.

Closure of the Cedes company brought its benefit in the shape of no. 9, but it created problems too: breakdowns could not be rectified, and with the majority of the ten-vehicle fleet out of action by the end of 1918, there was growing criticism of the transport authorities. The arrival of a new manager in 1921 brought a renewal of enthusiasm. Two years later the transport committee urged the modernisation of the trolley system. A Bill for conventional vehicles received the Royal Assent in July 1924; anticipating this, a modern Straker-Clough had arrived in the February, and the tram routes from Keighley to Utley, Stockbridge and Ingrow were equipped for ordinary under-running trolleybuses. A total of 18 Straker-Cloughs, eight single-deck and ten double, arrived up to 1925. All were equipped with BTH motors, and just one, no. 2, was left with Cedes gear for the Cross Roads service. The other Cedes routes

Page 125. (*left*) The last trolleybus bought for Bradford. (*above*) Bournemouth Sunbeam of 1936 which was converted to open top in 1958

Page 126. Incident. (*above*) Cardiff vehicle demonstrates the unsociable act of dewiring, while (*below*) Huddersfield 634 after 'missing' the Longwood turntable

had been closed and handed over to bus operation. One of the double-deckers, no. 58, was used with front-wheel drive mounted in a swivelling axle, an arrangement designed by G. A. Bishop who had a similar experiment running in Leeds. Keighley drivers, however, reported the vehicle too unwieldy; turning a corner required a fantastic number of pulls on the steering wheel. Cedes services were eventually finished off by the 1926 General Strike, Cedes vehicles having lost nearly £23,000 in 13 unlucky years.

Keighley's network was too small to be viable. Vehicles had a short working life, and it was estimated that re-equipping the trolley fleet could cost between £40,000 and £50,000. Instead, the joint Keighley-West Yorkshire Services Ltd took over in 1932, Keighley's last trolley running with the Mayor at the wheel on 31 August. The tolleybuses' downward path can be tracked as follows:

	Revenue	Net result
	£	£
1913–14	761	+ 284
1923–4	5,851	—2,242
1932–3	6,923	—5,163

RAMSBOTTOM

Local dissatisfaction must be have been felt too in Ramsbottom, where trolleybus services were never developed beyond a single route equipped with ancient-looking vehicles. The total fleet size of seven was made up in the first place with the usual 28-seater RET cars, with bodies by Milnes Voss and front entrances. Later, they were replaced by more single-deckers constructed in Leeds with Lockwood and Clarksons bodywork. Despite bus competition, this miniscule operation hung on until 31 March 1931, the original cross-centre Holcombe Brook-Edenfield service being progressively reduced.

MEXBOROUGH & SWINTON

Two services based on Mexborough started on 31 August 1915, one connecting the town with the Manvers Main Colliery, another running from Old Toll Bar, Mexborough, to Conisbrough, using Daimlers with Brush bodies. Services began at 5.30 am for the benefit of miners. Staff shortages soon presented a problem, and both routes were closed in 1917, Manvers Main reopening two years later, but Conisbrough stayed shut until 1922, when the original cars were replaced by single-deck AECs with solid tyres. In 1929, trolleybuses took over the route to Rotherham, vehicles travelling under corporation wires beyond Rotherham Bridge to the town centre. That established the basic T-shaped system, with Rotherham in the south, Mexborough at the intersection, Manvers Main on the left arm and Conisbrough to the right. That same year, Mexborough and Swinton took delivery of a Garrett single-decker, no. 31, a former demonstrator which had run in Birmingham. It was to earn praise during World War II as its reliability caused no spare parts headaches. Apart from the interlinked service into Rotherham, there were early suggestion of stringing up wire from Conisbrough to Balby and so on into Doncaster, but this came to nothing.

Maximum route mileage reached 24.27, and the company, part of British Electric Traction, was forced by the number of low rail bridges to stick to single-deckers. The last new batch of trolleybuses was delivered in 1948-9, when 33 Sunbeams with centre entrances entered service. They were in time for the record year, 1950, when the Mexborough network carried 16,661,000 passengers.

Abandonment had many causes in different places: around Mexborough it was the extensive development of new housing estates which required public transport. The first route replaced by buses was between Rawmarsh (Green Lane) and Rotherham. Final closure came on 26 March 1961, with civic guests being carried from Mexborough to Rotherham. Two 1948 Sunbeams involved in the closure ceremonies deserve particular mention. No. 29 was cut down specially to transport the Rawmarsh Brass Band to lend the occasion musical flavour; and no. 30 was one of the seven bought by Bradford and rebodied as double-deckers, that vehicle eventually becoming Britain's 'last trolleybus,' Bradford 844.

In their 45 years, Mexborough's trolleybuses had carried 382 million passengers and run 39 million miles: their passing was the last closure of a company-owned system.

TEESSIDE

This system, operating in some of the bleakest industrial landscape in Britain, was administered by an unusual co-operative agreement between local authorities, and was busy extending and modernising routes into the late sixties. The trolleys were run until mid-1968 jointly by Eston Urban District Council and Middlesbrough Corporation, which had a one-third share in the enterprise.

The wiring was first ready in February 1916, but service vehicles did not begin running until 8 November 1919, experimental operations having taken place the previous month. The first cars, all single-deck, were provided by

Cleveland Car Co, with English Electric bodies and Dick Kerr motors; another half-dozen vehicles were bought from the short-lived wartime network at Rhondda. In the spirit of the new traction, a complete 'internal' telephone system was installed connecting each terminus with the depot. For the trolleys a new bridge was constructed over the North Eastern Railway at South Bank a few yards from the depot at Cargo Fleet. The service was supplemented between 1924 and 1936 by a petrol-electric bus, developed by Tilling-Stevens Motors to connect Normanby with the village of Eston. The original cars were replaced in 1932 by 32-seat, four-wheel single-deckers from Ransomes. They were painted blue with a cream band, and boasted tinted glass which, on a gloomy day, must have made Teesside streets almost invisible! The first double-deckers did not arrive until 1944.

The depot at Cargo Fleet was unusual in that limited accommodation meant only trolleybuses could be stabled under cover; buses were left outside. Modern practice was in evidence at North Ormesby where equipment on the trolleys enabled them to change the traffic lights to ease operation at a cramped turning circle near a level crossing. The original hedge green livery eventually became an unusual eau-de-nil with silver lettering.

The layout with services from North Ormesby to Grangetown (Kingsley Road) and Normanby remained unchanged from 1951 until a burst of activity in the mid 1960s. It began in July 1964, when the wiring was extended from Kingsley Road to Fabian Road. The time seemed right, with receipts for the 1963-4 financial year up by £9,278, and the number of passengers by over 4,000. By this time, the fleet of double-deckers was 15 strong: purchasing new vehicles was becoming impossible and in 1965, no. 5, a Sunbeam F4, was rebodied by Roe in Leeds. It was the last time a British trolleybus was thus re-equipped, although the result was not a particularly modern-looking vehicle. In 1968, the fleet was significantly enlarged with the purchase of five Sunbeam F4As, with Burlingham bodies, from the Reading system. The need for new vehicles arose after 31 March 1968—the day before the County Borough of Teesside Transport took over from Tees-Side Railless Electric Traction Board—when wires were extended from Fabian Road to Normanby. The mile-long section was put in mostly to cut out the difficult Normanby turn-round by linking the two existing termini. The move, opposed by local bus operators, at last took trolleybuses through Eston itself, and was the last extension equipped in Britain. At the same time, redundant wiring on the spur to Grangetown Square was removed.

It had been intended to continue trolleys on Teesside until 1973, which would have robbed Bradford of its glory. But the 1969-70 winter was unkind;

serious operational difficulties resulted from the growing shortage of spare parts. Trolleybuses were cannibalised to keep a seven-strong fleet on the road. During the summer of 1970, the last change was made when the fleet was renumbered by having 'T' prefixes in front of the vehicle numbers. The end came on 4 April 1971, although special last runs for enthusiasts and official guests were staged on the 18th: so finished Britain's second to last system.

YORK

This historic city, so unlike most of Yorkshire's dingy prewar communities, dallied with trolleybuses in two separate experiments which never got close to founding a full-blown network. Intense motor bus competition in outlying districts eventually forced the municipal operator to merge transport services in an arrangement which left no place for trolleys.

Powers for trolley operation had been obtained in 1914, but it was three days before Christmas 1920 when York's four single-deck Railless vehicles ventured out on the route to Heworth. Because of the city's famous narrow streets, the vehicles were only 6 ft 3 in wide, and were equipped with front entrances for one-man operation. The narrowness did little to dispel their bulk—'They were heavy, cumbersome things,' recalls an observer. Apart from being lumbering tanks, these RET cars had a low life expectancy, and the system was shut down in 1929.

Trials were held later with a double-decker, a Karrier borrowed from Doncaster, where it had been numbered 22. Size predictably ruled this trolley out, so York ordered three single-deck Karrier E4s with Roe bodies for its reopening in 1931. The general manager at the time, R. S. Asher, seems to have been in favour of the trolleybus: he is on record that year as recommending to the transport committee that overhead wiring be installed to take passengers to the York City football ground. Trolleybuses were doomed though by the West Yorkshire Road Car Co, the same concern which had ended the trolleys' relatively brief reign in Keighley. The West Yorkshire had 'swamped' the routes operated by York Corporation outside the central area, and the financial difficulties which ensued led in 1935 to the forming of a joint committee. Five days into the year, York's second trio of trolleys were withdrawn at the same time as the last York tramcars.

HALIFAX

The story of this town is bound up with developments north of the border in Dundee, where, as we have already seen, a trolleybus system lurched along for a year-and-a-half before World War I. The two RET vehicles which had been used there were purchased by Halifax Corporation in January 1918 and renovated. The pair were expensive at £1,900, and the intention was to use them for carrying goods on the Continental pattern, rather than for passengers. Replying to objectors, the chairman of the town's transport committee said the corporation 'might have to go in for goods carrying, and as each of these cars would carry five tons of material at a time their use would relieve the number of heavy carts.' As noted, Bradford converted its original cars to electric lorries, but Halifax only used the vehicles for passengers.

The route chosen was the 2½ mile Pellon and Wainstalls section, a bleak moorland route. The Ministry of Transport inspecting officer was less than keen at the state of the road surfaces, but approval was forthcoming and trolleybuses went into service on 20 July 1921. Ironies begin here: the manager was soon blaming the poor roads for damaging the cars, the reverse of the position in Dundee where the same vehicles were held responsible for cutting up the surface! Three years later, a Tilling Stevens trolleybus with BTH equipment, which had been built by the Halifax tramways department, augmented the fleet.

In 1926, Walter Young was appointed manager. He had succeeded Peter Fisher as manager at Dundee, notable as Britain's first trolley closure. Mr Young was no admirer of trackless, and motor buses replaced the Halifax trolleybus trio after 24 October 1926.

WEST HARTLEPOOL

The inspecting officers of the Ministry of Transport, more often associated with investigations into railway accidents, were kept busy in the twenties checking 18 new trolleybus installations. Rarely did their findings cause problems, and their co-operation made much trolleybus development possible. Yet with the West Hartlepool system, they found much to criticise, and the first years saw three major clashes where the inspectors considered the municipality had fallen below standard.

The undertaking's first route to Foggy Furze was inaugurated on 28 February 1924, using four Railless trolleys with Short bodies, the vehicles being equipped for one-man operation. Two years later the Park service was equipped, and the corporation bought an open-top Railless double-decker for another route to the seaside suburb of Seaton Carew. At first the Ministry of Transport refused operating permission for no. 7, with its open cab and boom mounted on a column at the front of the vehicle. The route too, caused trouble because the poles were erected on the wrong side of the road. Seaton Carew finally saw trolleybuses on 28 March 1927; the open-topper was taken out of service a year later.

Another link wired up in 1926 was that northward into Hartlepool. A

Garrett and a Ransomes vehicle were hired for the Ministry inspection. A jinx had settled on the undertaking by this time, and the tolleys were repeatedly dewired. The inspecting officer would not allow service running until more span wires were put in. Once trolleys began running, 12 new Strakers went into the joint ownership of Hartlepool and West Hartlepool, carrying both towns' seals on the lower side panels. Twelve Garretts were supplied for the West Hartlepool area. After that, there were three more batches: in the mid-thirties, six Daimler double-deckers with Roe bodies and Metrovick equipment were purchased to replace the original trolleys and numbered 1–6; eight more Daimlers were delivered in late 1938 for the joint service; and in 1939, single-deckers were bought again, three Leylands with centre entrances for the Seaton route. Postwar, an order for more Daimlers was changed to buses, and the decline set in firmly in 1949 when the Seaton trolleybuses were cut. The fleet size settled down at 17, including three single-deckers, plus nine trolleys owned jointly with Hartlepool. The agreement with Hartlepool, always a source of friction, was finally discontinued, and the end for trolleys came on 31 March 1953.

WIGAN

The year 1925 was the busiest for trolleybus openings. Four new networks started up, and two of them were short-lived, with Wigan lasting only seven years. The town needed to replace narrow gauge trams on the Martland Mill Bridge route, and the main factor in favour of trolleys was the useful load they would provide for the municipal power station. Four Straker-Clough single-deckers were ordered with Brush bodies, and, at a cost of £8,305, the service was equipped and went into operation on 7 May. In a rash of enthusiasm, the corporation explained its policy: motorbuses were not wanted because mobility provided no distinct advantages. Apart from being a customer for the power system, trolleybuses were considered 'clean, reliable and easy to maintain.'

The usual malaise clinging to the majority of single-route, small-fleet networks was soon evident; a change of manager in 1931 brought a recommendation in the June to abandon. The policy was carried out after 31 October and motorbuses took over.

MANCHESTER, ASHTON-UNDER-LYNE & OLDHAM

The story of these undertakings is closely linked because of the joint operation of routes; indeed four more authorities can be brought in as well. Ashton started trolleybuses first, inaugurating a joint route with Oldham on 26 August 1928, Ashton supplying four Railless cars and Oldham two. Oldham's interest went back three years earlier, when a deputation from the town visited Wolverhampton network soon after its inception, and was impressed by the trolleybuses' 'smoothness.' On the recommendation of the current manager at Bradford, Oldham fitted its pair of 37-seat Railless with 'cushion' tyres, which were solids with serrated tread. The running qualities did not appeal to the Oldham authorities, and they ceased trolley operation after 13 months. Ashton continued to run its vehicles to the boundary at Hathershaw.

Manchester's trolleybus inauguration was not until 1 March 1938, after the usual wrangling and debate over figures and possibilities. Tram joint working with Ashton had been an important part of local transport, and trolleys continued the pattern. Manchester's transport committee was not over-enthusiastic, but ordering went ahead for vehicles and route equipment for the Ashton Old Road service, with a £117,000 depot being constructed at Rochdale Road. Seven of the 11 tenders received for six-wheelers were for £1,000 and seven out of ten four-wheelers were quoted at £995. An enthusiasts' handbook remarked years afterwards: 'The (transport) committee's comments at this evidence of a price ring are not recorded.'

Thirty-eight four-wheelers from Leyland and a similar number of Crossley six-wheelers were purchased. Gradual route expansion continued during the war. When the corporation decided to convert the Moston route, there was no time for a Parliamentary Bill to be submitted, but the Ministry Inspecting Officer gave emergency approval with the general manager having to take the relevant responsibility. Powers were eventually obtained in retrospect in 1946. In 1943, the route had been extended beyond Gardener's Arms to A. V. Roe's factory, where trolleys terminated in a private bus station during peak hours. As with the Birmingham wartime extension to the Rover works, the actual destination was gently concealed under the name 'Greengate.'

The joint services with Ashton were well integrated; either authority would 'rescue' a faulty vehicle belonging to the other if necessary. As a small idiosyncrasy, Manchester's trolleybus conductors were always known as 'guards.' Football crowds were catered for with the installation of a siding for the Maine Road ground in Lloyd Street South. At the other end of the system, Ashton's depot was ¼ mile from the nearest service route, and the depot overhead was separate from the wires outside, which meant 're-poling' a trolley entering or leaving.

By 1953, all of Manchester's network, using a fleet of over 250 vehicles, was in operation. That year, the last batch of new trolleybuses was ordered from British United Traction, the vehicles having Burlingham bodies and Metrovick equipment. Ashton declared its intention of going on with trolleys for ten

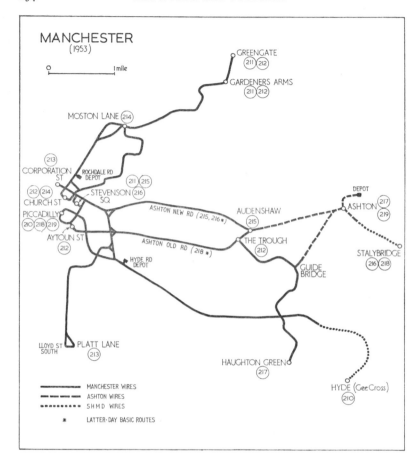

MANCHESTER
(1953)

years—it was to suggest abandonment in 1958, in fact—and the future was mapped out in a 10,000 word report by general manager A. F. Neal. It was prepared to support the decision to buy the 62 new 8 ft wide, 60-seat BUTs. He compared bus and trolley figures, calculating that the tax on fuel oil swung the balance in favour of the trolley, making them 1.293d cheaper to run per mile, or £30,195 in a year. Curiously enough, although the report gave trolley-buses the green light, it is rather pro-motorbus in many of its conclusions.

The year after the new BUTs arrived, Manchester started the downward path. It was planned to replace the Moston services, and close the 115-vehicle Rochdale Road depot. This was replaced by installing new wires in the other depot at Hyde Road on the 210 route. In other areas, though, services were being expanded, mostly to meet the demands of large new overspill estates at Haughton Green and Hattersley. The trolleybus in Manchester was doomed particularly by the fact that the city surveyor's department had always opposed the extension of routes into the main shopping streets: so the termini clung to the outer fringe of the central area. After October 1963, only three routes were left, the 215, 216 and 218, which traversed the Ashton Old and New Roads. The 216 and 218 were pooled as far as revenue and administration were concerned. At the eastern end of these services—as had been the case with the 210 to Hyde—the wiring was owned by a joint authority: Stalybridge, Hyde, Mossley and Dukinfield. The 215 terminated at the Audenshaw boundary and so was all-Manchester operated; the 218 was the preserve of Ashton vehicles after May 1966.

Other signs of shrinkage had come two years before when the all-night service on the 215X (the letter being used to denote short workings) was withdrawn. After August 1966, trolleybuses were discontinued on Saturdays. The end for both Manchester and Ashton came on the last day of that year, very little publicity being given for the trolleys' farewell.

DARLINGTON

No municipal motorbuses appeared on Darlington's streets until 1951, the tram stronghold having been invaded by trolleybuses on 17 January 1926. 'Darlington electricity,' as Stanley King has put it, 'consumed Durham coal: charity, it is said, begins at home.' The first trolleybuses were a batch of 20 Straker-Cloughs with Roe bodies and BTH equipment. They had centre entrances and set the trend for Darlington single-deckers until after World War II. The initial fleet was put on the Haughton Road service ostensibly to replace trams, but a shortage of trolleys kept trams busy for some time after their formal abandonment.

English Electric, Ransomes, and Leyland trolleys arrived, the last a batch of eight in 1937 still modelled closely on the vehicles delivered 11 years earlier. Rather more modern were nos. 64–7, Leyland TB5s, fitted with East Lancs bodies, which were bought in 1940. Later in the war, Darlington bought two dozen Karrier Ws with utility bodies. It was not until 1947 that moves were made to buy double-deckers. An order was placed with BUT, but initially the corporation asked to cancel the contract because it was expected the postwar Labour government was about to nationalise all public transport. Eventually, the threat of State control was lifted, and Darlington's fleet strength went to a total of 95 with the purchase of six double deck BUTs.

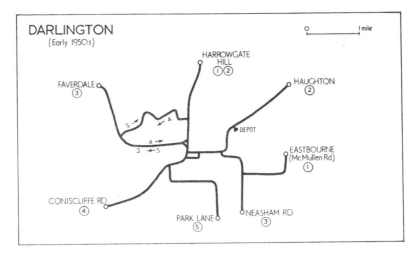

In a pattern encountered elsewhere, the purchase of a batch of expensive postwar trolleys was soon followed by progressive abandonment of the system; conversion to bus operation beginning in 1951. A year later, the almost new BUTs were sold to Doncaster, which, in 1962, passed six of them on to Bradford in the country's only thirdhand trolleybus transaction. Two factors had forced Darlington to dispose of its trolley fleet. In the first place, the underground feeder system had been inherited from the tram days, and the need to overhaul both the cables and the exterior overhead was urgent. The cost of re-equipping was put at between £60,000 and £80,000. Also, being on the main A1 road, lorries with high loads tended to arrive in the town unexpectedly, creating the danger of fouling the overhead wiring.

The Suez crisis, which created a serious fuel oil shortage, meant a reprieve for trolleybuses on the remaining service, route 3 between Faverdale and Neasham Road. This link succumbed to motorbuses on 31 July 1957.

GRIMSBY & CLEETHORPES

The fishing port of Grimsby and the seaside resort of Cleethorpes made unlikely partners for a public transport link; and as if to emphasise this, trolleybus operation in the two areas had its contrasts despite through running. Grimsby was the dominant partner, though, inaugurating its first trolley route on 3 October 1926, with a connection from Riby Square to Weelsby Road. It was another 11 years before Cleethorpes joined in, with a through route being opened on 18 July 1937. This began at Grimsby's fish-laden Old Market and ran into the centre of Cleethorpes and along the front to the holiday atmosphere of the Bathing Pool. The success of the operation was proved to the satisfaction of Cleethorpes authorities when it was found that receipts rose 26.8 per cent in the year following conversion.

Twenty years after the Cleethorpes start, it was decided that a full-scale merger of the two networks was sensible. To the passengers, the main evidence of this was the appearance on the vehicle sides of both towns' coats of arms, although the badges kept a careful two feet apart! Before the amalgamation, Grimsby operated 13 trolleybuses, mostly AECs and Karriers, with one old-style central entrance six-wheeler. The livery was maroon and white. Cleethorpes' grey and blue fleet had been nine strong, with AECs, a Crossley and up-to-date BUTs. After the merger, the livery was blue and cream, and one depot in Grimsby was retained. The overhead style was still noticeably different in the two parts of the system. As for routes, the 10 was the original Riby Square-Weelsby Road service; 11 was the joint route; and the 12 ran from either Grimsby or Cleethorpes to the boundary at Park Street, where there was a double turning circle.

A couple of years before closure, trolleybuses ceased appearing on Sundays, and gradually buses took over weekday workings too. Before the end on 4 June 1960, only eight trolleybuses were licensed, and for the final run of all, from Cleethorpes to the Grimsby depot, only three enthusiasts were aboard to mourn.

ST HELENS

The home of Britain's biggest glass-making business gained Parliamentary powers for trolleybuses in 1921 to serve a populace which, according to one local student of transport affairs, had always hated the town's trams. When services began between Rainhill and Prescot on 11 July 1927, single-decker Garretts were used, four of these Ransomes-bodied vehicles being ordered. After that, the Corporation showed its preference for Ransomes chassis, the firm supplying the first double-decker in 1931 after the South Lancs system extended trolley wiring to the boundary at Haydock, and through working began. Municipal trolleys on route 1 worked under South Lancs overhead as far as Atherton.

Gradually the town network grew until there were five routes including the Prescot circular. To expand the double-deck fleet, Leyland TBD5s with Massey bodies arrived in the thirties. The last of the reviled trams ran on April Fool's

Day 1936, and the last trolley extension was in 1943 when the Ackers Lane route was wired, having never had a tram service.

Two batches of trolleys were added to the fleet—which eventually reached 65 vehicles—during and just after the last war: first, 10 South Africa-bound Sunbeam MF2s were diverted to the system, and in late 1945 a similar number of Sunbeam Ws with wartime utility bodywork entered service to replace the early Ransomes double-deckers. The final deliveries were in 1950-1, when eight Sunbeam F4s and eight BUTs, all with East Lancashire bodies, arrived.

Despite the relative small scale of the operation, St Helens trolleys boasted a few odd features. The early red and cream double-deckers which appeared after the South Lancs opening carried side destination boards on the tramcar pattern. Although there were only five basic routes, a multiplicity of short workings meant there were over 20 separately designated services. Even though the trams had been short on popularity, they offered customers and everyone else the luxury of a postal service. Trolleybuses continued this feature (seen also in Bradford and Huddersfield) for about ten years, collection boxes being fitted at the back, and posting could take place at stops. In the town centre in the early days a one-way scheme was installed for the trolleys, one of the first examples of this method of traffic management.

A unique item of trolleybus equipment in St Helens was a device to prevent full-sized trolleys running under a low bridge in Peasley Cross Lane on the St Helens Junction route. The need arose after 1950 when the corporation bought its BUTs and Sunbeam F4s which were the first normal-height trolleys in the fleet. The Ministry of Transport Inspectorate expressed concern that one of these trolleybuses could accidentally be put on the Junction service: it was another problem taken up with alacrity by R. Edgley Cox, manager at the time. On the approach to the rail bridge, the overhead wires were spread and one lowered. If a highbridge trolleybus appeared on the route, its nearside negative boom would be depressed on to a roof-mounted electrical interlock, lighting up a 'Warning Low Bridge' indicator in the cab and cutting off power. It is worth recording that the emergency equipment was required just once— when the trial trolleybus with Mr Cox and the Ministry Inspector aboard arrived to check the system! The inspector was satisfied, but the trolleybus had to be hauled away backwards because no facilities for turning existed nearby.

Mr Cox was soon off to the Walsall system, St Helens having decided in 1950 to do away with trolleys. Four routes were axed in 1952, others following over the next four years. The Prescot circular carried on alone for two years. On 1 July 1958, the day after official closure, Sunbeam 374 made a farewell trip with a civic party.

DONCASTER

Narrow streets and traffic congestion made trolleybus operation in Doncaster difficult, and it is interesting that the problem of car parking led the corporation to obtain an Order, confirmed by the Minister of Transport in August 1935, banning parking in certain roads, one of the earliest examples of such restriction.

Trolleys were first proposed in 1921, but serious thinking did not begin for another four years, when the question of renovating the tram route out to Bentley was raised in talks with Bentley Urban District Council. A powerful argument in favour of continued electric traction was the need to provide a good load for the town's power supply, so trolleybuses began operating to Bentley on 22 August 1928. Equipping the route cost £12,990 and eight double-deckers came at £2,105 each. Revenue jumped 50 per cent, but the corporation was even more impressed during September 1931, when it found that replacement motorbuses put on because of flooding helped receipts up another 25 per cent.

Even so, a total of seven routes were speedily converted to trolleybuses, the last being the Balby service, opened in mid-1931. In all, over 70 vehicles were used in Doncaster, including Bristol E101, based on a three-axle motorbus chassis and shown at the 1929 Commercial Vehicle Exhibition. Postwar, the majority of the fleet comprised 30 carefully-maintained Karriers and Sunbeams with standardised Roe bodies. Even though Doncaster was not among the pioneers, the well-kept maroon trolleys were always known as 'trackless' vehicles.

Having got the network together in a month under three years, Doncaster concentrated on running an uncomplicated fleet. In 1953, closure of the system was almost ordered because of extensive road and bridge alterations, but the plan was deferred. That year saw the appointment as general manager of T. Bamford. A brochure written as trolleybuses were ending ten years later said that trolleys 'with their lack of flexibility, make town operation ... very difficult.' Yet in earlier years, Mr Bamford had argued the trolleys' case quite persuasively, once taking the 'inflexibility' argument itself to pieces. In the technical Press, he remarked that fixed routes were accepted. Diverting services to 'odd corners' of estates because of local pressure 'often succeeds in securing an unwarranted and costly deviation.' Mr Bamford also pointed out that keeping trolleybus drivers was easier, because having no public service vehicle licences, they could not be 'poached' by motorbus operators.

Flexible or inflexible, Doncaster's trolleybuses were doomed. The first withdrawal was that of the original route to Bentley on 13 February 1956, although this was due to bridge reconstruction. The final route abandoned was the Beckett Road service, which had been extended in 1958, a year which also saw route mileage added on the Wheatley Hills section.

Trolleybus interest did not die with the closure on 14 December 1963. Twenty vehicle bodies were transferred to diesel bus chassis, the conversion to half-cab specifications being done by Roe, the original maker. One particular body was stated to have completed 653,000 miles as a trolleybus before becoming a bus.

SOUTH LANCS

This is the last of the few company-owned trolley systems we shall encounter, and the South Lancashire Transport Co had a habit of doing things its own eccentric way. Ten six-wheel Guys with lowbridge Roe bodies were purchased for the beginning of services on 3 August 1930. Highbridge vehicles followed in 1936, although nos. 48–51, Roe-bodied Leylands, were actually owned by Bolton Corporation. After the first few years, these trolleys were used on the supplementary Leigh-Atherton-Mosley Common run, and Bolton local services were worked by company vehicles.

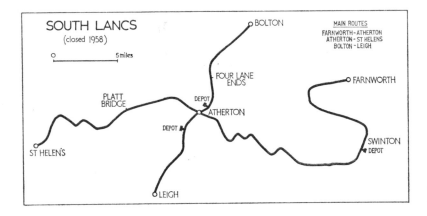

South Lancs operated three basic routes, each with a clearly defined character. Totally ignoring crow-flying techniques, the route between Farnworth and Atherton straggled around for 14 miles, travel being complicated by a long layover at Swinton, where through passengers were required to rebook. For the first $1\frac{3}{4}$ miles out of Farnworth, the local urban district council owned the wires and leased them to the trolley operator. Cramped streets meant that trolleys had to use single line sections in Tyldesley and Atherton. From Atherton to St Helens ran a separate service, interworked with St Helens Corporation via the town boundary at Haydock. On the way, trolleybuses cut off a corner at Platt Bridge by using a ¼mile private roadway. Originally it had been a reserved tram track, and during heavy rain, SLT trolleys would bump and splash through the puddles clustering around the old rails.

A similar arrangement to that at Farnworth applied for the first three miles of wire south from Bolton to Four Lane Ends, which was the property of Bolton Corporation. The route continued south by way of Atherton to Leigh. To underline the differences between South Lancs routes, their descriptions in the timetable were as follows: Atherton-Farnworth was served by Trackless Trolley 'Buses; Bolton-Leigh was a Trolley Vehicle Service; and Leigh-Mosley Common was a Trolley Bus Service.

South Lancs got its mileage out of the vehicles used: the 1930 Guys survived for nearly 30 years. Those who knew the system treasure the memory. The vehicles, although fairly modern in appearance outside, were 'pure 1930s' within. The only postwar additions were six Weymann-bodied Sunbeams acquired in 1948. No route numbers were carried, destination being indicated by a cryptic word or two in a single-line box. Overhead wires were sometimes secured to a convenient tree if the relevant traction pole had rusted into disuse. The manager's house at Atherton adjoined the SLT power station, so his home was dc-powered direct.

In November 1946, Bolton Corporation had sent a deputation to inspect the Portsmouth installation to help make 'a decision on the trolleybus.' One eventually came ten years later when Bolton local services were replaced by motor buses, and Bolton's four trolleybuses were taken to the town prior to scrapping. They went to the corporation's depot to be seen there for the first and last time. The rest of South Lancs, with elderly vehicles and overhead, only lasted another two years, trolley services ceasing on 31 August 1958. The next day, local dignitaries travelled by special trolleybus from Atherton to Leigh, then on by bus to a celebration lunch in Wigan. But the trolley was more or less incidental, the occasion being mostly to mark Leigh's participation in a replacement joint bus service. For a while, though, Atherton's power supply stayed on to feed a waiting room and inquiry office.

HUDDERSFIELD

Remaining aloof from the excitements nearby over trolleybus development before World War I and in the twenties, Huddersfield waited until 1933 before beginning the routes which wound out of the town and up to the blustery moors which fringe it. Six different vehicles were purchased for the inauguration of the Almondbury service on 4 December 1933. Three of them were Karriers, two with Park Royal bodies and the other by English Electric, and there was a Ransomes D6, a Sunbeam, and an AEC.

Karriers evidently demonstrated the sturdiness required for the hilly area, and these were in the majority of batches ordered up to 1940, mostly with Metropolitan-Vickers equipment and Park Royal bodywork. Important route extensions came after the first year, when trolleys appeared on services to Outlane and Lindley. Outlane had the distinction of being the highest trolleybus terminus in Britain, standing 954 ft above sea level at the edge of the moors. Equally exposed to the elements was the turn-round at Longwood, terminus of the 40 and 41 routes from Bradley. Here, a turntable was built on a platform set into the hillside. Actually turning the equipment as in Christchurch proved too hazardous in windy conditions, so trolleys simply reversed on to it. As we shall see later, the arrangement still presented dangers. Three of Huddersfield's routes were on hills steep and long enough to warrant the fitting of coasting brakes.

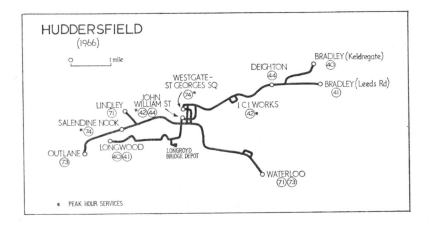

The fleet size reached a peak of 140 vehicles in 1940 and 1947. In all, 14 routes were converted to trolley operation. In one case, trolleybuses were turned short of the original tram terminus of Honley, mainly because of a low railway bridge at Lockwood. The last tram conversion was in 1940 with the equipping of the Brighouse service, taking the mileage to a shade under 36.

Page 143. (*above*) Last trolleybus built for Britain, Bournemouth 301. (*below*) Christ-church's famous turntable plays host to Reading 174 during an enthusiasts' tour

Page 144. (*above*) Leeds experiments with a battery bus just after the final abandonment at Bradford, and (*below*) preserved trolleys gather at Sandtoft Transport Centre

The depot was at Longroyd Bridge, just off route 40, which, appropriately enough, had originally been a generating station for the tram layout.

After the second war, the fleet was systematically rebodied, the last new batch delivered—Sunbeam S7s with East Lancs bodies and Metrovick motors, purchased in 1959—was the last for six-wheel trolleybuses in Britain. Huddersfield's livery underwent a steady metamorphosis from chocolate and cream to the same colours plus red, eventually ending up a straight red and cream. The system was ahead of the field in the use of two-way radio to make overhead repair work as efficient as possible. H. Muscroft, general manager in 1949, recommended that four tower wagons should be so equipped, the only problem being the hilly character of the district which created a few 'blind spots' in reception.

The first reduction in mileage came as early as 1955, when the Brighouse route was pruned to Fixby. Closure of the West Vale service in 1961 and Marsden two years later was caused by the expense of maintaining overhead outside the corporation boundary. Actually, the first contraction preceded the last extension: this was to Bradley's Keldregate terminus, opened in 1956 and in use for 11 years. The original Almondbury route went in July 1965, and the final route left in operation was the 71 and 73 from Waterloo to Outlane and Lindley, which went on alone for a year. The last trolleybus to run was BUT 623, built in 1956, which took the usual dignitaries on a cruise round on 13 July 1968.

NEWCASTLE

Like Darlington on a bigger scale, the onus was on Newcastle to find ways of burning coal, and this factor kept route extensions coming along until 1950. The city's distinctive yellow and cream fleet was influenced to a large extent by the somewhat similar vehicles borrowed from Bournemouth during the war, which persuaded the corporation to fit rear entrances and front exits as standard. Otherwise, the large number of BUTs purchased in postwar years looked remarkably like London trolleys, although the sight of vehicles crossing the high Byker Bridge—paralleling the span carrying the Tyneside electric trains, which have followed the trolleybus into obscurity—would be difficult to repeat with the capital's more modest structures.

With words from the Lord Mayor, trolleybuses began in Newcastle on 2 October 1935, on the 9.6 mile run from residential Denton Burn to the shipbuilding centre of Wallsend, a route which covered part of the line of Hadrian's Wall. Thirty vehicles were ordered to start the service. There were AECs with Metropolitan-Cammell and Weymann bodies, Guys with English Electric bodies, and Brush-bodied Karriers. Inspectors reported the drivers 'slow and nervous' in the first few days, with frequent dewirements and as much as five minutes added to the running times. After four weeks, however, operation was very smooth, and in the November, 25 more trolleys were ordered to meet the demands of an expansion programme. The only knotty problem was the embarrassing destruction of street lights connected to the overhead, which blew out when the early trolleys used heavy regenerative braking.

On 19 September 1937, the Denton Burn route was joined by that from Brighton Grove to Walker, the service being extended to Denton Square six months later. An indication of the lighter use of public transport in an area of hardship was the fact that trolleybuses on this extension ran only at 20-minute intervals, halved in peak periods. The same year, the Fenham route was opened, and trolleys began running from the centre to Osborne Road and the Wallsend boundary. It was on Osborne Road that wartime Newcastle put to work a batch of trolleys hired from Brighton, five of those delivered standing spare. Nine others were obtained via London from Bournemouth, five being licensed from 1 October 1942, and the rest after 1 December. Three of the trolleys were passed on to the neighbouring South Shields network. More trolleys were bought from Bradford at the end of November, six going into service. Three were described as 'odd types' and stored, and one, Bradford 595, an all-English Electric of 1931, was described simply as 'not usable.'

A dozen wartime utility vehicles were purchased for the opening on 11 June 1944, of trolleybus services on the old Elswick Road tram section; it was over three years before the next extension, when the Osborne and Elswick Road termini were linked. Thereafter, there was a flurry of activity by a corporation impressed at the average gain in receipts following trolley conversion of between 25 and 28 per cent. An important Sunday was 18 April 1948, when one of a batch of 20 new 8 ft wide Sunbeams took the Lord Mayor and the Sheriff of Newcastle on a new cross-boundary route to Gosforth Park Gates, where they met representatives of Gosforth Urban District Council. About that time, the pressure to make new conversions with motorbuses was growing, but the general manager, Frank Taylor, was opposed: he pointed out the need to conserve dollar reserves and talked of the 'probable world shortage of oil' some 20 years before the expression 'energy crisis' became widely used.

At the beginning of November 1948, four routes were allocated, and seven more followed the next January. The last Newcastle-owned trams were phased out in 1950, with the Heworth-Wrekenton route being replaced by buses, the Gateshead-operated tram service to Saltwell Park being superseded

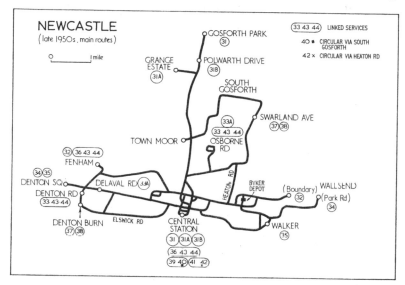

by buses in March 1951. In the October, Haymarket depot ceased to be used by trolleybuses, and the 100-strong fleet was concentrated on Byker.

The decade of the fifties was a time of consolidation before the first closures in the mid-1960s. Routes were numbered in the 30s and 40s, and the system included one of the least-used sections of trolley overhead in the country, the route to Town Moor, operational only during Race Week Fair. Most termini were equipped with reversers, and on at least one occasion, between May 1958 and the following April, a temporary reverser was erected at Hadrian Road while a rail overbridge was rebuilt in Park Road, Wallsend.

The first cut came in June 1963, when the 34 route across the city from Wallsend to Denton Square was replaced by buses. Five more routes were abandoned eight months later, including the Gosforth Park section. Another seven followed in May 1965. Service 35 from Denton to Walker survived another 17 months until the final shutdown on 2 October 1966. Four years later, the Tyneside Passenger Transport Executive was formed, but it was instructive that its Newcastle routes which had replaced trolleybuses duplicated almost completely the trolley layout. The pte, under dynamic management, was to create a stir in the next couple of years by promoting a new 'super tram' scheme.

SOUTH SHIELDS

The Tyneside PTE also embraces South Shields, which had opened with trolleys a year after Newcastle, but only ever operated a fleet something like one-sixth the size. The curious point about South Shields was its resemblance in many respects to the Bradford network—indeed enthusiasts knew it as 'Bradford by the Sea.' Two ex-Bradford officers went to the town as managers in the thirties, and their influence was seen in the blue and cream livery and in the roadside stops and signs, all pure duplicates of the Yorkshire pioneer.

The first trolley ran on 12 October 1936, when the Mayor drove Karrier 200—most of the fleet was to consist of Metrovick-powered Karriers—from Market Place to Fremantle Road, the frequency soon being increased from every twelve minutes to every nine. The next year, trolleybuses travelled on to Marsden Inn, and a new route was inaugurated from Market Place to Stanhope Road via the depot at Chichester, unusual in that it was on two levels because of the gradient of Dean Road.

Tram replacement proceeded with the extension of trolley wiring ¾ mile from Market Place to the Pier Road, and the other way to Tyne Dock. The layout allowed two basic circular services to be operated, one 'inner' and the other a fairly complex 'outer' figure-of-eight. In July 1938, it was decided to tap the seaside traffic along the South Foreshore by extending the overhead along the Coast Road to Marsden Bay. Another ¼ mile was added the next summer to allow trolleybuses to reach Marsden Grotto, where the corporation levelled a piece of ground for a turning circle. This route was very exposed, and as well as damage to fittings by corrosion, traffic was light except in the height of the holiday season.

During the war years, four interesting secondhand vehicles were taken on, three of them, appropriately, from Bradford. Two were 1931-2 English Electric six-wheelers withdrawn in 1947; the third Bradford trolley was the front-entrance AEC Q type of 1934, which went to Tyneside in 1942 as no. 235, taken out of service nine years later; the last was the only single-decker in the fleet, Bournemouth's unique Thornycroft, which ended up in decrepit state in a local fairground. New connections to the important dockside area were opened in 1942 from The Lawe, the site of a Roman encampment which overlooks the whole town. The new Tyne Dock services were for workmen only at first, but became all-day routes with link-ups being constructed to Horsley Hill. No trolleys ran along the Coast Road from the outbreak of war until June 1944, because of emergency restrictions. The last trams were replaced to Ridgeway from the beginning of April 1946.

The major postwar conversion was that from Horsley Hill Square in the centre of new housing development, via Westoe to the Market Place, for which a dozen new vehicles had been ordered. The gap between Horsley and Marsden was closed the same year, 1948, when trolleybuses ran on to Marsden Inn, the wiring itself being extended along Radwell Lane to join the coastal route at the original Marsden Bay terminal. Marsden Inn-Market Place was operated as a circular on the town's usual pattern and became the most lucrative route, numbered 11 and 12 when numbering was introduced in 1949.

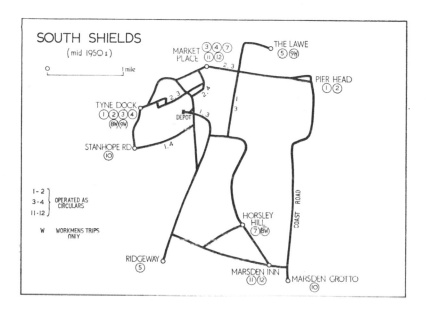

In April 1952 the workmen's service connecting Tyne Dock with Horsley Hill was withdrawn as unremunerative. As a reflection of local working conditions, it is interesting that trolleys on this route and the 9 worked mornings, evenings and in the middle of the day to transport workers intent on going home for lunch. The Coast Road service came to an abrupt end in February 1958. A severe snowstorm started on the 8th, soon blocking the exposed route, and it was decided to put on buses after the 10th.

The next year, work began to enclose completely the lower part of Chichester depot, so for ten months, 31 trolleybuses were parked at night along the side of the King George Road dual carriageway. A nearby civil defence underground headquarters were converted into a temporary control centre for services. About this time, the idea of abandonment was kicked around, but met resistance in a Labour-dominated council concerned for miners' jobs. The first major withdrawal came in 1961 with the cutting of services 5 and 9 to The Lawe. No. 7 from Horsley Hill and the 11 and 12 Marsden circular disappeared on 16 May 1963, leaving South Shields with its original circular links. These finished on 30 April 1964. There was no ceremony, and few passengers were aware of the impending changeover to buses. Indeed, it is recalled that the driver of the last trolley, which entered the depot at 11.20 pm, was not aware of the historic moment!

HULL

Several features of the Kingston upon Hull network were unique, probably the most noticeable being the determinedly Continental style of the vehicles. Trolleybus operation had been turned down by a town's meeting in 1930, but minds changed, powers were obtained in the summer of 1936, and Cottingham Road garage was equipped with trolley overhead. The first service was opened from King Edward Street to Chanterlands Avenue North on 23 July 1937, service running beginning tow days later. As the network expanded, Hull established the principle of not giving the destination, just descriptions like 'Via Holderness Road,' and so forth. Route numbering was in the 60s and 70s and replacement trolleybuses often turned short of the original tram termini, the result of service co-ordination with East Yorkshire buses.

The first vehicles ordered were 26 Leylands with Weymann bodies, joined in 1938 by 20 Crossleys with Craven bodywork. During the war, when services were often disrupted by the heavy air attacks mounted on the city, two batches of Sunbeam W utility vehicles were purchased, and more Sunbeams followed up to 1948, by which time the fleet had grown to its peak of 100 vehicles, based on four garages.

The last new service had been added in 1945 with the route from Waterworks Street to Dairycoats completing the 14-mile trolleybus map. Significant alterations in the look of the system began in 1953 with the delivery of trolleybus 101, a dual-entrance Sunbeam MF2B with a Roe body, resplendent in the livery of azure blue and white, lined out with black to give a streamlined appearance. The vehicle was exhibited at the 1952 Commercial Vehicle Show. Two years later, no. 102, first of a batch of 15 more MF2Bs, was the trolleybus 'star' of the 1954 Show.

Yet the slick new vehicles, complete with trolley retrievers, could not conceal a shaky future. The sharp decline in passenger carryings in the early sixties persuaded the transport department to prepare a scheme for one-man operation, using the MF2Bs and possibly some single-deckers, but union agreement proved difficult and abandonment proposals overtook the project. The first to go was route 70 the 1945 extension designated 'via Hessle Road' in the peculiar Hull tradition. Trolleybuses were replaced by buses on 28 January 1961 on the Dairycoats run. The last service was the 63 from Chapel Street to Beverley Road (Endike Lane) which disappeared on 31 October 1964.

	Revenue £	Passengers	Trolleys	Buses
1946	609,151	88,293,181	84	145*
1949	721,002	102,069,738	100	157
1952	832,031	89,947,878	100	152
1955	902,124	82,085,017	90	158
1958	925,860	78,245,133	86	153
1961	1,075,041	70,287,805	63	165
1964	1,258,217	65,721,656	16	219

* including 18 trams until 31 March

GLASGOW

The tramcar dominated the only Scottish municipality apart from Dundee to try the trolleybus, and only in Glasgow could the fear have been expressed that trolleys would 'involve greater risks than fixed track vehicles.' Since 1898, a huge fleet of electric trams had been built up; trolleybuses in fact got consideration first in 1921 when it was suggested they would be ideal vehicles to link outlying areas with tram termini. The project was defeated at a public inquiry after route proposals had been published in 1933.

As World War II ended, the need to provide work for the corporation's Pinkstone power station led to new plans being announced for trolleybus trials on the Provanmill-Polmadie tram route. The £126,000 cost would include 20 vehicles. As the ideas coagulated, it was decided to order 34 BUTs and Daimlers with MCW bodies, similar to London's postwar Q1 class and vehicles being delivered to Newcastle. Indeed, Glasgow even adopted the 'Trolleybus' bullseye sign used by London Transport, although the badge was withdrawn after objections by LT. The first Glasgow route, 101, began on 3 April 1949. It was Britain's last new trolleybus installation, 37 years and 10 months after the Bradford and Leeds inaugurations. The first vehicle in use was TB2, which travelled from Larkfield Garage—like Hull, the city never used the expression 'depot'—to Riddrie, becoming dewired on the way. It was the first such incident in a long line, and eventually, to try and overcome the problem, TB1 was fitted with a unique single boom and diverging head. Having been shown at the 1952 Commercial Show, the device lasted just a week in service. The trouble was ascribed largely to electric frog operation, and as a result all Glasgow's overhead pointwork became mechanical. When route 102 between Riddrie and Polmadie started, trolleybus deliveries were lagging behind schedule and so motorbuses had to be used initially. To supplement Larkfield garage, another was opened at Aikenhead Road in December 1950. The four-acre site, dominated by the Hampden Park football ground, cost £53,000 to equip. No overhead was erected, trolleybuses manoeuvring under battery power. Hampden garage had a capacity of 135 trolleys. Govan and Dennistoun garages were shared by trolleys after 1958, providing storage for another 73 vehicles; Larkfield, which was also a bus garage, taking 58 trolleybuses.

Destination screens carried route numbering up to 120, but actual services stopped short at 108, with the last service replacing trams between Paisley Road Toll and Mount Florida in 1958. The basic principle was that trolleybuses should use segregated roads in the centre. Where trolleys and trams did run together (Glasgow was the last place where this could be seen) trolleys were not allowed to overtake the lumbering cars. Another hazard was the amount of horsedrawn traffic which persisted in Glasgow after most municipalities had forgotten the nuisance.

Vehicle design underwent a radical development in 1950 after E. R. L. Fitzpayne, the general manager, had visited Stockholm for the International Union of Public Transport's conference. He came back convinced that maximum-capacity, standee vehicles could answer prevailing problems, and so TB35, later TBS1, was constructed. It was a BUT single-decker with MCW body and Metropolitan-Vickers equipment. The conductor was seated and there was space for 27 passengers (reduced to 26 when the conductor's section had to be enlarged) and 40 standing. Ministry of Transport permission for one year's trial operation was given. The vehicle was exhibited at the 1950 Commercial Show, and studied the following year by delegates attending the International Union in Edinburgh. It was the only time a trolleybus ran there, using the trams' positive overhead wire, and a trailing skate in the Princess Street tracks. TBS1 was also seen at Atherton on the South Lancs network, and when TBS2-11 were built, Nottingham and Walsall tried one of the batch out. It was a brave experiment. The conductor could issue instructions with a microphone and a 'STOPPING' sign would illuminate at the front of the saloon when the brakes were applied so the standing passengers could brace themselves. The standee trolleybuses were used on the 101 and 102, but were never a great success. They were allowed no longer en route than other vehicles, and tended to lose an average of two minutes during peak hours because of slow loading. The corporation found it was difficult to persuade passengers to move on to the platform in a body, and few got the hang of having fares ready. All were reconverted between 1959 and 1961: the fact remains they were the forerunners of a whole range of urban transport vehicles in use today with less passenger aids.

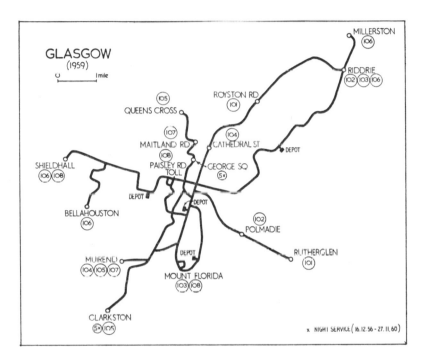

Meanwhile, trolleybus operation in Glasgow was showing reasonable returns. In the year to 31 May 1950, it was reported that trolleys made a £3,000 profit, against losses of £150,000 by the bus fleet and a massive £309,000 deficit by the trams.

Pessimists got their first warning in 1954 when some trolley wiring in Adelphi Street was dismantled. However, vehicle innovation was not finished: two-axle 30 footers were supplied in October 1955, by BUT; and then 34 ft 6 in single-deckers with 50 seats were provided for the 108. Unique in Britain, this second batch was on BUT export chassis and had Burlingham bodies.

The city's 195-strong trolleybus fleet always played a minor role in transport generally, and the 1958 sale of the Pinkston power station to the nationalised electricity authority for £1 million was the long-term signal for the end. The first trolleybus deficit in 1961-2 was big enough to cause concern at £88,547. By 1964-5, the trolleys' losses had risen to £268,000, against a £165,000 loss by the 1,400-strong bus fleet. Routes 103 and 104, as well as the short-lived night trolley 5, had gone before 1966 the year when the original 101 and 102 routes as well as the 106 were axed. March 1967, saw the end of the 107 and 108, leaving only the north-south 105. The last official trolleys ran on 27 May 1967, when two double-deckers and a single-decker journeyed to Hampden garage. A curtain call was arranged, however with TB 123 making a short run out the next day to allow photographs.

*   *   *

Few Corporations in the North did not put up at least a few miles of over-head and try trolleybuses. One exception was Preston, ironically enough the home of English Electric, where much trolleybus equipment was made. The town's tramway committee had recommended the spending of £27,830 on a fleet of 20 vehicles and the conversion of the 3¾ mile Penworth-Farrington route. This came to nothing, but a trolley was seen on the streets in the autumn of 1929, when one of the all-EE vehicles built for Bradford was operated with trailing skate over some of the tram routes.

CHAPTER SEVEN

BELFAST

THE surge of interest in trolleybus traction in the twenties and thirties took a long time to cross the Irish Sea, and when it did, only Belfast, the capital of Northern Ireland, adopted the system. It is intriguing that even Belfast may have rejected the notion of trolleys had not Westminster intervened in the city's transport affairs in an unforeseen way. Not long before powers to run trolleys had been granted in 1930, a new manager was appointed, William Chamberlain. He had just come from Leeds where no secret was made of his preference for motorbuses over the pioneer trolleybus network there. In 1928, Mr Chamberlain had withdrawn the last of Leeds' outmoded trolley vehicles. It is hard to say what his view of Belfast's needs would have been, for no sooner had he arrived than the authorities in London offered him a post under the 1930 Road Traffic Act as first chairman of the Traffic Commissioners for the North West Traffic Area of England, and, reluctantly, Belfast Corporation had to let him go. He was knighted in 1939, dying at the age of 64 five years later.

It was left to a successor, Major Robert McCreary, to usher in the Belfast trolleybus. The 1930 powers had been sought by the corporation which had succeeded in making accelerated repayment of loans on new tramcars and tram equipment. A study of existing trolleybus schemes was instituted and in 1936 a deputation visited various English authorities. It was decided the Falls Road route would be the best choice for a test bed. It was 3½ miles long, the existing tram track was the most dilapidated on the system, and there was a convenient depot in Falls Road itself. This was equipped for eight trolley 'tracks' and seven experimental vehicles ordered from all the major suppliers were delivered there. The 68-seat bodies, with a livery of dark blue and creamy white—later to be replaced by maroon—were constructed by Harkness, which equipped the growing fleet regularly after that. The first batch cost £2,670 each. There was obviously a good deal of scepticism that trolleybuses would not catch on, for the *Transport World* reported on 14 April 1938: 'If the service proves unsatisfactory they will be hauled back and a refund obtained of £1,000 on each vehicle.' The Falls Road service had been operating for 17 days by the time those gloomy words appeared, and there was every indication that the venture was a complete success.

On the first day, the Lord Mayor, Sir Crawford McCullagh, drove the last Falls tramcar from Castle Street to Queen Street where he and other civic guests boarded the first trolleybus. Perhaps he was one of the sceptics, for he chose the occasion of the opening ceremony to make some remarks about Northern Ireland's poor position in public transport financing compared with the rest of Britain. He told his audience at Belfast Castle that taxation was '27 per cent higher on trolleybuses in Ulster than England.' He made the point more graphically with a thoughtful example: if all Belfast's trams were to be replaced at that time by trolleybuses, the cost would be £10,000 more than an English fleet of equivalent size. It would not be much consolation to Sir Crawford and his ratepayers, but from the operator's point of view, being in Ulster did present some advantages, with greater latitude being allowed for vehicle width and ground clearance.

At the end of the first year, trolleybuses on the Falls route had shown a £9,847 surplus over working expenses. A suitably impressed corporation then agreed to plans for a complete changeover to trolleys by 1944 at a cost of £1.25 million. But this scheme and the delivery of a second batch of trolleybuses were severely delayed by the outbreak of war in September 1939.

Nevertheless, the equipping of new services did continue, the Cregagh and Castlereagh routes opening in 1941, and Stormont and Dundonald the following year. The 22 and 23 route to Stormont had a unique character. Having ventured out from the gloomy city, the trolleys would pass through the gates of Stormont and then make a long loop of the elegant parliament building itself. Because of the area's importance, wartime restrictions prevented photography, although a handful of shots were allowed of vehicles coming through the gates, taken by contractors who had equippped the overhead. The war did sharply reduce the flow of new equipment—the complete tramcar conversion programme was eventually finished ten years late—but caused a tremendous increase in business. Belfast was dotted with vital shipyards and aircraft factories. The number of passengers carried in the 1944–5 financial year was 257,906,582, nearly double the 135,647,992 in 1938–9. The figures apply to trolleybuses, trams and buses.

Once the war was over, seven years were spent installing new trolley routes in the following order: Bloomfield, opened in May 1946; Ormeau, April 1948;

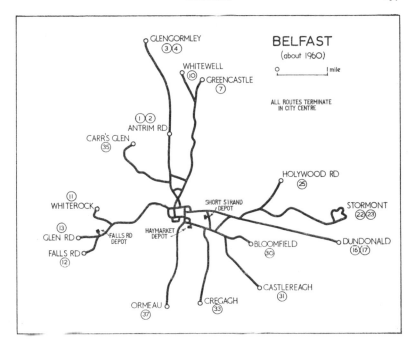

Glengormley, January 1949; Greencastle, October 1950; Carr's Glen, April 1951; Glen Road, April 1952; Holywood Road, November 1952; and Whitewell, April 1953. The fleet grew to 245 vehicles, including AECs, Guys and Sunbeams. The AEC design was the most popular, fitted with GEC equipment. Compared with other systems the traction motors were relatively low-powered, those produced in the late 1940s giving a balancing speed of 31.4 mph. This was considered by the corporation to be 'entirely suitable' for the heavy urban traffic and large number of stops.

The original Falls Road depot became too small for the expanding fleet and was closed for service duties on 4 May 1947. Trolleybuses were transferred the following day to the Haymarket depot where most of them were parked in the open air. Falls Road continued to handle major vehicle overhauls. Pressure on space was always severe, and another depot was planned at Short Strand. The site had been bought in 1940 for £10,750 and cleared, but it was the old story with the war holding up the necessary materials. When hostilities were over, a ready-made depot was found in the shape of an aircraft hangar at Kilkeel, outside Belfast. It had a 120 ft span and was 240 ft long. The corporation transport department bought the hangar for £3,000 and took on workers from the famous Harland and Wolff shipyard to re-erect it at Short Strand. It was Belfast's first fully equipped depot for rubber-tyred vehicles. One problem was that of heating the structure, but this was solved by installing underfloor equipment. The depot opened in October 1950, although it was not used by trolleybuses right up to the end of services in 1968. Apart from the one-time hangar and the tour of Stormont, Belfast boasted a few other features, including a trolleybus siding at York Road station so vehicles were ready to transport boat train passengers arriving from the port at Larne. Another siding was located at the Crusaders football ground.

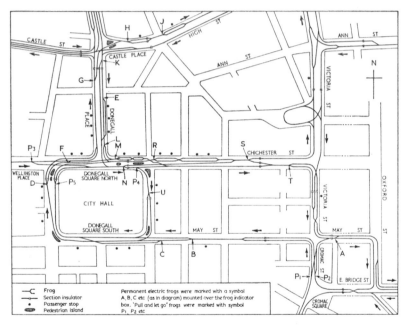

Britain's most complicated stretch of wiring—the City Hall area of Belfast after July 1958

The most important development in Belfast came in the city centre, where the introduction of new traffic flow arrangements in 1958 necessitated a complete upheaval of trolleybus overhead and working. The Corporation's electrical engineer at the time was Robert Adams, later to become general manager. He was an ardent trolley man, and the scheme, which would turn out to be the most complicated stretch of wiring in Britain, was his 'baby.' The accompanying map shows his grand design complete with the three parallel sets of wires sweeping round one of the corners. Apart from yards of new wire, 145 new poles were required to supplement conveniently-sited existing ones. Material for the project cost £23,459, and the labour came to £9,691. The difficult part was the need to train crews to thread their vehicles through the wiring and the traffic. Each driver sat through a two-hour lecture addressed by Mr Adams. Drivers were also issued with a fairly complicated 36-page manual describing the movements, stops and frogs to be operated as trolleys negotiated the various routes. The manual provides a fascinating documentary record. The introduction by J. C. McClelland, chief traffic officer, and Mr Adams includes the following:

'Trolleybus drivers are reminded that to get the best advantage from ONE WAY traffic operation careful attention should be paid to taking up position in the correct traffic lanes in good time before coming to junctions and turns.

The overhead wire system has been laid out to afford trolleybus drivers the best opportunities possible to maintain their correct position in the traffic stream.

A most important feature of ONE WAY traffic working is that of vehicles "WEAVING". This means vehicles effecting movement from one side of a street to the other side to take up station in the proper traffic lane while proceeding along, and in doing so not inconveniencing other vehicles . . .

In conclusion it should be emphasised that while every possible step is being taken to ensure that the changeover on the 20th July next will take place smoothly, easily and without trouble this result can only be achieved if everyone concerned makes certain beforehand that they fully understand the new system and its method of operation.'

As an example of how the manual was used, these were the instructions for trolleys turning at Cromac Square heading for Cregagh, Bloomfield, Dundonald, Holywood Road and Stormont:

Street	Operation
Cromac Street	On arriving in Cromac Street from East Bridge Street operate frog P2. Weave over to the right hand side of the road. Turn right into May Street.
May Street	Drive on the centre of the road. Operate frog A and weave over to the left hand side of the road to the stops.

The rewiring was carried out by Clough Smith with A. G. Ratcliffe in charge. it had been scheduled for the previous weekend, but Mr Ratcliffe vetoed the idea when he learned that a traditional Orange march was to be held in the city then. The work was completed without disturbing traffic on the weekend night of 19-20 July. The first morning, transport officials held their breath as the power was switched on and trolleybuses appeared ... all went well, except for one direction indicator showing a false setting at frog B. This was corrected within five minutes. The general manager, J. Mackle, wrote later in a letter of reference for Clough Smith that the layout was a 'masterpiece of organisation' allowing as it did for 20 route permutations. But there were grumbles among local residents who objected to the forest of traction poles.

One poetically inclined reader of a Belfast newspaper spotted the disappearance during the reorganisation of an inspector's hut, and he sent in the following letter:

> *'Sure, they've gone and moved our kiosk*
> *From its site in Castle Place,*
> *But this doesn't make me wonder,*
> *For it was a rank disgrace.*
> *Then they said: "Where shall we put it*
> *Just to keep our buses right,*
> *And offer our inspectors*
> *Some small shelter in the night?"*
> *So they got a million steel poles,*
> *And they stuck them round a square*
> *With a million miles of trolley wire*
> *A-swinging in the air.*
> *So, if you want our Lord Mayor,*
> *I'll tell you where to call.*
> *He's at Britain's biggest bus stop*
> *The kiosk's the town hall.'*

Most of the trolley fleet were six-wheelers, but 25 four-wheelers had also been bought. In 1959, an up-to-date two-axle Sunbeam, no. 246, had been purchased and was intended as the forerunner of a replacement fleet. The same year, route 11 was extended along Whiterock Road. But there had already been some closures, and the last tram routes had been converted to bus operation in the mid-fifties. As well as 246, the corporation took delivery of a one-man-operated Leyland Atlantean bus, and this was to show the way ahead.

Before 1959 was out, the decision was made to abandon the trolleys ultimately. The trolleybus was contributing well to city funds at the time: in 1959-60 trolleys made £86,110 of the total £109,186 surplus. The undertaking incurred losses until 1964, but trolleybuses managed a £13,000 surplus in 1963.

The pace of abandonment was quickened in January 1961, when minutes of Belfast Transport Committee disclosed that it was not planned for trolleys to cross a new bridge over the River Lagan. The Queen Elizabeth Bridge, to provide an 'outward' flow paralleling the old Queens Bridge, was to be a steel span structure with concrete decking. The manager's suggestion of providing pole sockets for possible operation fell on deaf ears. The Stormont and Dundonald routes were affected, and they shut in March 1963. An enthusiasts' party made a special Saturday visit to mark the closure of the Stormont service 21 years to the day after its inauguration.

Various upsets affected the latter days of trolley operation. On a Saturday in July 1960, services came to a halt after a trolleybus driver was dismissed because a woman claimed she had lip read offensive remarks. In October 1962, 22 drivers and conductors struck for four hours on the Glengormley route after evening service frequencies had been cut from five to six minutes, generous indeed compared to modern conditions. Ulster's troubles are known world-wide now: on 14 August 1965, 'political disturbances' were blamed for broken windows in a number of trolleybuses on the Falls, Glen Road, and Whiterock routes. The following month, Belfast Trades Council claimed that the 100 remaining trolleybuses were in a 'dangerous condition' and urged public service vehicle testing. They must have been surprised to hear from the corporation that trolleys were regarded administratively as light railways! The official last runs were on 11 May 1968, a Saturday. Three trolleybuses, including the 11-year-old 246, carried a civic party from City Hall to Falls Park. Councillor John Harcourt presented the Lord Mayor with a trolleybus bell, just as his father had done on the last tram on 27 February 1954. There was something a little Irish about the ceremony, for actual last runs were made for passengers on the Glen Road, Whiterock and Whitewell services the next day. And the final run of all was made by an enthusiasts' group, whose trolley slipped into Haymarket depot just after midnight on 13 May. 'The trolleybus's cardinal virtues of cleanliness and silence were lost sight of and it had to go,' commented a transport department brochure rather paradoxically.

H.B.T.B.—K

CHAPTER EIGHT

INCIDENT

APART from the ordinary hazards faced by all vehicles in crowded streets, trolleybuses had particular troubles of their own, although it must be said that their accident record throughout the country during 61 years was exceptionally good.One problem which remained well-nigh unresolved throughout the whole trolleybus era was that of dewirements, when the booms would lose contact with the overhead and spring upwards out of control. Bamboo poles, carried generally under the trolley and retrieved from the back of the vehicle, had then to be used to haul the offending boom down by hooking the end of the pole into a loop below the collector head. Sometimes, dewirements could have serious results if the trolley head flew off. Even if the head remained attached, a flailing boom could wreak havoc with the overhead, and there was inevitably a delay to traffic as the trolleybus was 'rewired.'

Chaceley Humpidge, then general manager at Bradford, reported in 1952 that 'trolley dewirements from all causes average 1.25 per 10,000 miles,' while another manager, T. Bamford, who had supervised the Maidstone installation before moving to Doncaster, put together some interesting ideas on dewirements in the *Bus and Coach* of September 1954. He had shared the view that lengthening trolley heads to provide more contact with the wire was a partial solution. Most heads varied from 64 to 94 mm long, but he experimented with 125 mm. The result was quite successful, but a side effect was the excess load on the overhead.

Mr Bamford was an advocate of curve segments on bends rather than span wires, adding: 'Crossings and frogs are the cause of fewer dewirements than is the general belief, mainly because of the relatively low speed at which these are taken.' The rule was to limit speeds through junctions to 5 mph. He pointed out that section breakers, where there was a short rigid section of wiring, could cause boom 'bounce' and thus possible dewirement; and a heavily cambered road surface was also a hazard for a trolleybus. He produced one fascinating technical point: if as a trolley passed under a span wire at 25 mph it was dewired, the driver had three-and-a-half seconds to brake hard and stop to avoid striking the next span with the errant boom. 'The importance of the correct driving of the vehicle cannot be overestimated,' he declared. Mr Bamford quoted the old trolley driving aphorism: 'Right shoulder under the wire.' Fierce braking and acceleration were reprehensible; careful notching-up and positioning were all-important. In later years, it was common to hear officials complaining about the driving standards of young employees, an increasing number of whom drove their own easily-manoeuvrable cars when off duty.

All operators took dewirements seriously, and when one was reported, immediate checks would be carried out on the relevant stretch of overhead. As an example of staff discipline, Bradford drivers whose vehicles dewired had an interview with a chief inspector, and persistent offenders faced demotion to conductor. Hull, Bradford and St Helens tried trolley retrievers at various times, but although widely used on the Continent, such equipment found scant favour in Britain.

A tragic dewirement occurred in Bradford in August 1970, involving an Allerton trolley at Four Lane Ends. The booms left the overhead violently, one snapping as it struck a lamppost. The broken part fell and hit two little brothers aged six and four who were sitting on a bench at the side of the road. Both died. At the subsequent inquest a transport official stated that a faulty frog was to blame. Unfortunately, the next day the boom on another trolleybus travelling along St Enoch's Road had broken, smashing a window in the vehicle. The incidents were completely unconnected, and it could be argued had nothing to do with the vehicles' basic design. Yet when general manager Edward Deakin announced final withdrawal a week later, it was not a good time to argue the trolleybus's merits.

We have already seen the dangers faced by passengers on the early open-top Cedes vehicles. But, in fact, nobody is recorded as having been injured by the hazardous collection equipment. However, an accident in Keighley in August 1920, underlined the difficulties of using outmoded systems. To reach the depot in Utley, vehicles would be 'uncoupled' from the overhead and allowed to coast down St John's Road. The driver of no. 9, the original Hove demonstrator, went upstairs to detach the Cedes collector—his conductor appears to have forgotten to sprag the wheels. No. 9 careered downhill and plunged into a garden. The driver was hurled out but not badly hurt. A contemporary newspaper picture shows the vehicle upright but facing downwards at a 45° angle, with little evidence of damage. The trolley returned to service a week later.

On conventional trolleybuses, the current collection apparatus on the roof created a high centre of gravity, and this made overturning more likely. A double-deck bus being put through the classic 'tilt test' had to go over to an angle of 28°—with a trolley, 25° was sufficient, recognising the top-heavy nature of the vehicle. Single-deck trolleys had to tilt 32° against 35° for a single-deck bus.

Trolleybuses showed their propensity for capsizing early, when the first enclosed double-deck, Bradford's 15 ft 4 in high no. 521, overturned in 1920 the year it was built. Little is known about the crash itself except that the driver was at work again the next day. A thoroughly detailed account of such an accident was given in 1938, when A. C. Trench, a Ministry of Transport inspecting officer, reported on the overturning of a Huddersfield Karrier on the Outlane route. The trolley, no. 12 in Huddersfield's fleet, was descending a gradient of about 1 in 15 during 'a storm of wind and rain of exceptional violence' on 4 October. Emerging from the shelter of houses, the vehicle was caught by a gust, skidded across the road, mounted a low bank and turned on its side, the brakes having failed. The only two passengers were slightly hurt and the driver suffered severe shock. The inspecting officer found the driver had stopped earlier to ask an inspector's advice because air pressure had fallen too low and the brakes were ineffective. The inspector and driver agreed to carry on cautiously to avoid inconvenience to passengers. In fact, the brake compressor had an intermittent failure caused by a badly-fitting fuse. The inspecting officer criticised both men. He noted that electric braking on the Karrier was provided on the power pedal only; he commended the increasing use of a righthand, partially-rheostatic pedal, which if applied, cut power to the other pedal. He made the point because the driver probably pushed his left foot down on the power pedal to try and keep his balance as the vehicle heeled over.

It hardly needs saying that the foregoing proves that no matter what the design of vehicle, any 'accident' is in reality due to someone's negligence. On 15 December of the year before the Huddersfield accident, a trolleybus on London's 696 route was involved in a spectacular smash on icy Wickham Lane, Plumstead. Braking to avoid a car, the trolley swerved across the pavement, uprooted a tree, crashed through a wall and fell 10 ft on to its side in the front gardens of three houses. Nineteen of the 30 passengers aboard were taken to hospital as well as the driver and conductor. Bank Holiday Monday 1939, saw Maidstone's only serious trolleybus accident. Having skidded at two previous stops, no. 29 skidded again as it was descending Stone Street and overturned in the mouth of Knightrider Street. The Ministry Inspecting Officer blamed the slippery state of the road.

The only major crash in Brighton occurred on 1 November 1950, when corporation vehicle no. 7 skidded on a wet surface on Carden Hill, hit a pile of gravel on its offside and went over. Two of the 23 passengers hurt were detained in hospital. Still in the south east, Reading 126 collided with a traction pole and overturned in Oxford Road on 27 March 1952. It never re-entered service; ironically, it was stored in the just-opened Whitley depot, and was sent away for scrapping when the depot closed six years later.

Bradford with its relatively large fleet had a spate of overturnings in the fifties and sixties. Two ambulances were called to the scene when trolley 599 overturned and blocked the Toller Lane carriageway while working the Duckworth Lane route on 8 September 1953. Only one passenger was injured when no. 753 on service 30 to Bingley hit a parked car and overturned on its offside on 26 July 1960. On the second to last day of 1961, no. 639 hit a lamp-post in Sticker Lane and overturned, smashing the driver's cab to matchwood. Severe damage was also sustained by vehicle 802 (purchased from Brighton where it had been no. 49) when it pitched over on 1 July 1963. Only the crew were aboard; the front axle was wrenched off and the offside front bodywork wrecked.

Newcastle's trolley fleet was remarkably accident-free until 13 February 1959, when no. 612 on route 33 turned over just after leaving the Benwell Lane turn-round. The vehicle had collided with a traction pole. Five passengers and the crew were hurt, the driver being dragged semi-conscious from his cab. Then, on the last day of September 1960, the driver of vehicle no. 546 was injured when the trolley struck a pile of gravel and overturned in Northumberland Street.

An unusual accident, due in part at least to the unique fixed turntable at Huddersfield's windswept Longwood terminus, happened on 12 February 1967. As already noted, trolleybuses had to reverse on to the turntable which was built on a projecting platform. No. 634 slipped off the turntable as it went backwards and rolled on to its side down a 15 ft drop. The driver was slightly hurt and the conductor was freed from the trolleybus unconscious. The vehicle had to be scrapped.

The driving instructions reproduced in Chapter Two stressed the dangers of running a trolleybus in the intermediate, resistance notches. In fact, there were several occasions when resistors heated up to the point where a vehicle actually caught fire. During the early years of the war, the combination of 'pea soup' fogs and the blackout forced all vehicles to run unusually slowly for long periods, and at least two undertakings, London and Huddersfield, had trolleybuses burn out when resistances overheated. Later on, two Glasgow trolleys were similarly destroyed during bad weather conditions in the winters of 1958 and 1959.

The old system of running trolleybuses under single tram wires by trailing a skate in the tram rails for negative current return produced its own hazards. Trolleybuses on Birmingham's original Nechells route had to reach the Washwood Heath depot by this method. During September 1940, a trolley arrived on the premises while fitters were changing a fuel tank on a motor bus. The trailing skate jumped out of the track and the resulting arc ignited the petrol . . . fortunately prompt action by the transport department's fire fighters prevented a serious blaze. Enthusiasts who chronicle the Bradford system report an unusual accident in May 1934, when an English Electric double-decker suffered a severe short circuit. It seems that molten insulating material cascaded on to the driver's head, causing him to lose control, and the vehicle hit a traction pole.

One enemy of the trolleybus was snow and slush, which would cause insulation problems, and many a passenger got slight electric shocks from handrails and so on during bad weather. Trolleys would have to be withdrawn wholesale from the streets, and braziers lit beside vehicles back in the depots to dry them out. During the severe winter of early 1963, Newcastle and South Shields were particularly badly hit. During January, South Shields trolleybus fleet was replaced by buses for three days, due mostly to overhead insulation problems. Flooding too presented trolleys with major problems, as electrical gear failed easily if soaked. Many of Nottingham's trolleys were immobilised in the summer of 1954 following exceptionally heavy rain. A few months later, operators noted with approval the trolleybus motors displayed at the Commercial Motor Show which were flood-proof.

The biggest bugbear of all, particularly in the late forties and fifties with Britain in the grip of austerity conditions, was the likelihood of power failures. These cuts were deliberate, but the possibility of breakdown was ever present, particularly at peak hours when demand for electricity would be heavy from all consumers. Generally, minor failures took between half-an-hour and an hour to rectify. In February 1936, in the days when power systems were the responsibility of local authorities, Bradford's trolleybuses suffered a failure lasting an exceptional four days. A typical example of a serious failure was in Harrow Road, London and occurred on a Saturday in May 1955. Service frequencies were very high on this stretch, and the breakdown stranded a $\frac{1}{4}$ mile queue of trolleybuses. Obligingly, passengers helped crews push 'dead' trolleybuses clear of busy road junctions. On 14 December of the same year, 55 extra motorbuses had to be drafted into service in Newcastle when the power failed for $4\frac{1}{2}$ hours.

CHAPTER NINE

END...AND BEGINNING

THE shortcomings of the trolleybus were not recongised only in the postwar years when the private car arrived in numbers which emphasised the trolleys' inflexibility. As far back as November 1908, almost three years before the Bradford-Leeds debut, Ernest Hatton, general manager of Newcastle Corporation tramways, declared at a meeting of tram operators· 'The independent unit has enormous advantages over any trolleybus system.'

Traffic congestion made matters progressively worse; but in the 1950s, something of a rearguard action was fought in several quarters on the doomed trolleys' behalf. An influential voice was that of Ben England. In February 1957, when he had charge of 155 trolleys and 283 buses at Nottingham, he complained in *Bus and Coach*: 'Had any government wished actively to foster trolleybuses in the national interest, it could have swept away the archaic legislation which controls the obtaining of Parliamentary powers for the installation and operation of trolley buses and for the very important matter of their subsequent extension.' Concessions, when they came, were too late to assist the bulk of postwar trolleybus development: in 1962, any route extensions could be carried out under a Procedure Order, rather than a Confirmation Order which had to be confirmed by Act of Parliament.

The same journal which published Mr England's remarks had urged the British Electricity Authority seven years earlier to offer a standard low rate for traction current 'fixed for a reasonable period.' Instead, the opposite was tending to happen. Indeed, there is general agreement among former operators that the electricity supply position, altered dramatically by nationalisation in 1947, was the key factor in the decline of the trolleybus. State ownership ended the old convenient arrangement whereby trolley or tram was a good customer for a local authority's power station, for instance, consuming 'off peak' current in useful quantities; a situation present-day electricity boards are trying to foster with electric storage heating and so forth. A thought-provoking

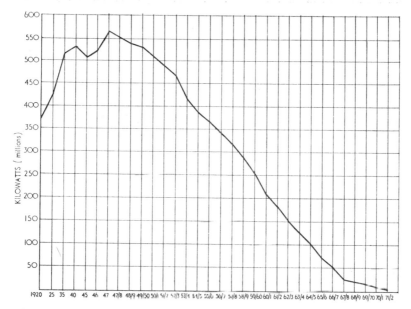

Electricity sales for street traction (including trams)

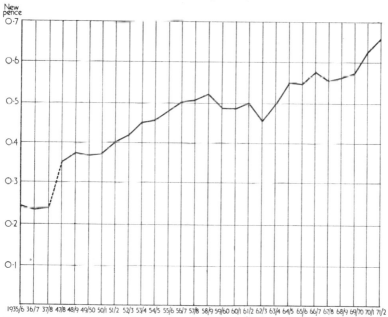

Revenue per kilowatt sold for street traction. Source: Electricity Council

view of the problem was presented in the Electricity Council's own magazine in July 1967, when it was declared that the electricity supply network had never been tailored to suit the essentially 'parochial' needs of a trolley system. 'In contrast,' wrote Philip Honey, 'every kind of oil-driven vehicle becomes a customer of the nationwide oil industry and particularly the public service vehicle for which oil is supplied in bulk.' He went on: 'When it is a matter of choice between oil and electricity the oil industry can spend so much more time and money presenting its case. The trolleybus, for example, has been practically eliminated from Britain's roads by the skilful propaganda for the diesel bus.' London's abandonment decision, he noted, was an important influence, although London switched power supply to its extensive Underground system.

The preceding graph shows how trolleybus and tram produced a steady rise in street traction electricity consumption, until 'peaking out' in 1947 itself; the sharp decline during the sixties needs no further explanation. It is worth noting that domestic consumers in 1920 took 271 million kilowatts, and this had risen to 70,413 million in 1971–2; electric railways accounted for 36 million kW in 1920 and 2,211 million kW in 1971–2.

Rationalisation among vehicle builders narrowed the postwar operators' choice. A lack of Government lead on trolleybuses' place in public transport was blamed for manufacturers' increasing reluctance to quote for orders; it became understood that a minimum of 50 new vehicles for any fleet was desirable. By 1956, 80 per cent of trolleys being built in Britain were for export, mostly based on long 'transit' chassis intended for single-deck bodies. With Sunbeam having supplied the last trolleys for Britain with the 1962 Bournemouth order, British United Traction completed its last order for any operator with a 1967 batch for Oporto, Portugal. After that a few chassis marketed by Scammell were provided for New Zealand trolleybuses. Although BUT as an entity had ceased manufacture, Leyland supplied trolley chassis to Arnhem, Holland, in 1969. Another sign of contraction was the withdrawal in the mid-sixties of the British Insulated Callender's Cables group from the supply of overhead fittings, the work being passed on to Brecknell, Willis of Somerset, a firm descended from Edward Munro's early overhead equipment business. The personality and professional training of individual managers was a major factor in retention or otherwise of trolleys. One newly-appointed manager at a south coast town was heard to declare: 'I never thought I'd live to see the day when my name appeared on the side of a trolleybus.'

Most of Western Europe has tended to adopt the diesel bus, although Switzerland's electricity-oriented towns remain faithful to the trolleybus, 136 new vehicles being on order at the end of 1972. Russia is another safe haven, and huge increases in trolleybus usage are predicted. Remembering to treat Soviet stastics with caution, the figures are:

	Length of single line (kilometres)		No. of vehicles		Percentage of total volume	
	Moscow	Rest of USSR	Moscow	Rest	Moscow	Rest
1940	198	400	563	—	7.6	3.4
1962	567	3,820	1,584	6,852	2.4	13.6
1980 forecast	—	24,400	—	48,800	—	22.5

Trolleybus development in Russia has been spectacular: in mid-1959, an articulated trolley went into service in Moscow with space for 200 passengers (seated!), seven doors, and with an overall length exceeding 55 ft.

As for Britain, vague hopes were being pinned on a single-deck electric battery bus as Bradford's last trolleys vanished. It was ironic indeed that one of these buses was being tried out in Leeds at the same time as the city's neighbour ended the trolleybus era. A pair of these pollution-free vehicles were designed for the Government by a South Wales company which became wholly owned by Hawker Siddeley after August 1972. Trials were also held in Liverpool and Sheffield. Costing about the same as a conventional double-decker, the battery bus could carry 26 passengers (nine seated and 17 standing) up to 25 mph. Maintenance costs were put at 0.2p per ton mile against 3p for an ordinary bus. However, the range of the batteries for a fully-laden vehicle in city centre traffic would be only 35 miles, and so the old problems of recharging were basically unaltered.

For the future, bands of enthusiasts are determined to enjoy those reminders of the trolleybus's past which remain. Ghosts of one sort and another abound. A few months after Bradford's March 1972, abandonment, tracing the original route there and in Leeds was worth the effort. Most of Bradford's first 1911 route south from Laisterdyke remained little altered, although the Dudley Hill terminus had vanished under a jumble of roundabouts, dual carriageways and pedestrian subways. Nostalgia was easier in Leeds. The Aire Street-Thirsk Row terminus adjoining City Square still looked capable of 'launching' trolleybuses out along Whitehall Road, where the flavour of the original, sparsely populated route lingered. Farnley was still bleak; the Woodcock Inn at the country turn-round had been rebuilt in modern style but the low wall in front was unaltered from the early pictures. Two traction poles, probably originals, stood beside the spacious cross-roads which could accommodate a a convenient turning circle. Back in Bradford, in a field adjoining the Tong cemetery terminus, lay the dilapidated teak-framed body of no. 515, one of the 'second generation' single-deckers built in 1914. It had been used as a shed, but still discernible were the tram-style side panels, driver's compartment, and metal roof fittings in the saloon. One one side of the stubby body ran the fading information: 'R. H. WILKINSON. GENERAL MANAGER.' No. 515 had been converted into a snowplough in 1929 and withdrawn soon afterwards.

With the growth of interest in disappearing forms of transport, trolleybuses have found a whole new group of friends, enthusiasts willing to help buy withdrawn vehicles. Relatively new trolleybuses were sold for tiny sums until the early 1960s, when operators woke up to their potential value. In October 1963, Belfast Corporation reported it had carried out an examination after vehicles which had cost £7,000 new were going for £25-£30. The scrap value was found to be more like £100, and so preservationists had to dig deeper into their pockets.

While systems still operated, running preserved trolleys under other wires became popular. In 1968, five years and five months after London's final conversion, LT no. 260, of the C2 class, ran in Reading. The same year, Derby 215 ran at Crich tram museum in Derbyshire, using the single wire and a trailing skate. It was the first time a trolleybus had operated on museum premises, and it was the start of a new trolley era. At Sandtoft, a former RAF airfield near Doncaster, the British Trolleybus Society and local groups have set up a transport centre, where in 1972, 22 trolleybuses were stored many of them under cover. Among the early arrivals was one of Epsom and Ewell's public conveniences, destined to be returned suitably to proper trolleybus order. A great day for Sandtoft was 3 September 1972, when Bradford 845 made the first public trip under specially-erected overhead. The trolley raised a cheer as it travelled 50 yd, driven by R. Edgely Cox, the ex-Walsall manager, who had talked earlier in a speech to guests at Sandtoft's open day of the 'beloved trolley vehicle.'

In the nearby village, an old chapel had been converted into the unlikely home for three beautifully preserved trolleybuses owned by the BTS chairman, schoolmaster Michael Dare. Inside was Reading 144, built in 1949; a Derby vehicle of 1944 in its wartime condition, with grey roof, wooden seats and no rear lights; and Manchester 1344, delivered in 1955, which attracted police attention when on one occasion it managed 60 mph.

A dozen trolleybuses had been taken to another museum site at Carlton

Colville, near Lowestoft, run principally by the East Anglia Transport Museum Society, the Historic Commercial Vehicle Club and the London Trolleybus Preservation Society. The trolleybuses—including three London vehicles and one of Bournemouth's final batch of Sunbeam MF2Bs—share the centre with trams as well as historic cars. Compared with preservation of railway vehicles trolleybuses are relatively inexpensive to purchase, but the ancillary equipment required for running is not. A one-ton drum with 1,542 yd of overhead wire cost £1,400, and even at scrap value would be around £500. Workers at Carlton Colville also found that a traction pole could cost £5 or £8, a figure doubled when transport costs were added.

A couple of individual preservation efforts were particularly interesting. The oldest trolleybus to be restored was Keighley's no. 5, one of the town's early double-deckers, which had ended up as a weekend bungalow near Grassington. The chassis was in near-perfect condition, and, having put the top deck back in position, Bradford stalwart Stanley King and friends were rebuilding the trolley, aiming at keeping 50 per cent of the original vehicle. There was no intention of making it operational, but, painted crimson lake in the tram style of the twenties, no. 5 was destined for a private motor museum. Around the time Bradford's last trolleybuses finished, members of the National Trolleybus Association acquired Hastings 45, one of the original Guy single-deckers supplied for the inauguration of services in 1928. It had been withdrawn in 1948, but after 1953, the vehicle (minus traction motor and cab fittings) was used as a booking office and waiting room at Hastings coach station. In March 1973, on the eve of the anniversary of Bradford's closure, Bradford 844, the country's official last trolley, was formally handed over to enthusiasts and towed to Sandtoft.

About 100 service trolleybuses have been preserved, and it is to be hoped that a fair number can become reasonably operational on museum layouts. The following list of saved trolleys is based on one compiled for Robert F. Mack, with certain additions, mostly to take account of the large-scale purchase of ex-Bradford vehicles during 1972.

Operator	Fleet No.	Chassis type	Date	Body type	Owners
Ashton	80	Crossley Empire	1950	Crossley	LTPS
Ashton	87	BUT 9612T	1956	Bond	LTPS
Belfast	98	AEC 664T	1942	Harkness	Belfast City Museum

Operator	Fleet No.	Chassis type	Date	Body type	Owners
Belfast	112	Guy BTX	1948	Harkness	Belfast Transport Museum
Belfast	168	Guy BTX	1949	Harkness	NTA
Belfast	183	Guy BTX	1949	Harkness	TMS (I)
Belfast	246	Sunbeam F4A	1958	Harkness	LTPS
Bournemouth	202	Sunbeam MS2	1935	Park Royal	NTA
Bournemouth	212	Sunbeam MS2	1934	Park Royal	BTS
Bournemouth	246	BUT 9641T	1950	Weymann	R. S. Cromwell
Bournemouth	286	Sunbeam MF2B	1959	Weymann	LTPS
Bournemouth	297	Sunbeam MF2B	1962	Weymann	Bournemouth Corporation
Bournemouth	299	Sunbeam MF2B	1962	Weymann	TMS (I)
Bournemouth	301	Sunbeam MF2B	1962	Weymann	BPTA
Bradford	706	Karrier W	1945	E. Lancs (1960)	BTA
Bradford	713	Karrier W	1945	E. Lancs (1960)	BTA
Bradford	731	Karrier W	1946	E. Lancs (1959)	BTA
Bradford	735	Karrier W	1946	E. Lancs (1959)	BTA
Bradford	737	Karrier W	1946	E. Lancs (1960)	Bradford Corporation
Bradford	746	BUT 9611T	1949	Roe	D. Mitchell
Bradford	758	BUT 9611T	1951	Weymann	D. Mitchell
Bradford	792	Karrier W	1944	E. Lancs (1958)	BTA
Bradford	834	BUT 9611T	1949	E. Lancs (1962)	BTA
Bradford	835	BUT 9611T	1949	E. Lancs (1962)	BTA
Bradford	843	Sunbeam F4	1948	E. Lancs (1963)	BTA
Bradford	844	Sunbeam F4	1948	E. Lancs (1963)	BTA
Bradford	845	Sunbeam F4	1950	E. Lancs (1962)	BTA

Operator	Fleet No.	Chassis type	Date	Body type	Owners
Bradford	846	Sunbeam F4	1950	E. Lancs (1963)	BTA
Bradford	847	Sunbeam F4	1950	E. Lancs (1963)	BTA
Brighton H & D	6340	AEC 661T	1939	Weymann	LTPS
Cardiff	203	AEC 664T	1941	NCME	BTS (on loan to LTPS)
Cardiff	243	BUT 9641T	1955	E. Lancs	NTA
Cardiff	262	BUT 9641T	1949	Bruce	Cardiff Trolley-bus Group
Cleethorpes	54	AEC 661T	1937	Park Royal	EMTS
Cleethorpes	63	Crossley Empire	1951	Roe	NTA
Copenhagen	5	Garrett 'O'	1927	Garrett	LTPS/NTA
Derby	172	Sunbeam W	1944	Weymann	M. Dare
Derby	175	Sunbeam W	1945	Park Royal	EMTS
Derby	215	Sunbeam F4	1949	Brush	Derby Trolley-bus Group
Derby	224	Sunbeam F4	1952	Willowbrook	EMTS
Derby	237	Sunbeam F4A	1960	Roe	EMTS
Doncaster	375	Karrier W	1945	Roe (1955)	Doncaster Omnibus Society
Glasgow	TBS 13	BUT RETB/1	1958	Burlingham	Glasgow Corporation Museum
Glasgow	TBS 21	BUT RETB/1	1958	Burlingham	NTA
Glasgow	TB78	BUT 9613T	1958	Crossley	BTS
Grimsby Cleethorpes	159	BUT 9611T	1950	N. Coach-builders	F. Whitehead & M. Smith
Hastings	34	Sunbeam W	1947	MCW	LTPS
Hastings	45	Guy	1928	Ransomes	NTA
Huddersfield	541	Karrier MS2	1947	Park Royal	NTA
Huddersfield	619	BUT 9641T	1956	E. Lancs	WRTS
Huddersfield	631	Sunbeam S7A	1959	E. Lancs	WRTS
Ipswich	8/16	Ransomes	1926	Ransomes	ILTS

Operator	Fleet No.	Chassis type	Date	Body type	Owners
Ipswich	41	Ransomes	1929	Ransomes	EAT Museum
Ipswich	44	Ransomes	1930	Ransomes	British Rail
Ipswich	56/58	Ransomes	1934	Ransomes	ILTS
Ipswich	126	Sunbeam F4	1950	Park Royal	ILTS
Keighley	5	Straker	1924	Brush	Keighley Corporation
Liege	425		1932		J. Moxon
London	1	AEC 663T	1931	UCC	London Transport
London	260	AEC 664T	1936	MCW	LTPS
London	796	Leyland	1938	MCW	Paris Mus. Society AMTUIR
London	1201	Leyland	1938	MCW	LTPS
London	1253	Leyland	1938	Leyland	London Transport
London	1348	Leyland	1939	Leyland	TMS (I)
London	1521	AEC/MCW	1940	MCW	LTPS
London	1768	BUT 9641T	1948	MCW	London Transport
Maidstone	52	BUT 9611T	1948	Weymann	H. Taylor
Maidstone	56	Sunbeam W	1944	Roe	A. Stevens
Maidstone	72	Sunbeam W	1946	N. Coach-builders	Maidstone Munipal Museum
Manchester	1250	Crossley Dominion	1952	Crossley	EMTS
Manchester	1344	BUT 9612T	1956	Burlingham	BTS
Newcastle	501	Sunbeam S7	1948	NCB	Newcastle Corporation
Newcastle	628	BUT 9641T	1950	MCW	LTPS
Nottingham	466	Karrier W	1945	Brush	EMTS
Nottingham	493	BUT 9611T	1948	Roe	EMTS
Nottingham	502	BUT 9641T	1949	Brush	EMTS
Nottingham	506	BUT 9641T	1950	Brush	WRTS
Nottingham	578	BUT 9641T	1951	Brush	EMTS
Notts & Derby	353	BUT 9611T	1949	Weymann	NTA
Notts & Derby	357	BUT 9611T	1949	Weymann	EMTS
Portsmouth	201	AEC 661T	1934	English Electric	Montagu Motor Museum

Operator	Fleet No.	Chassis type	Date	Body type	Owners
Portsmouth	313	BUT 9611T	1951	Burlingham	NTA
Reading	11	AEC 661T	1939	Park Royal	BTS
Reading	144	BUT 9611T	1949	Park Royal	M. Dare
Reading	174	Sunbeam S7	1950	Park Royal	M. J. Russell
Reading	181	Sunbeam S7	1960	Park Royal	M. J. Harvey
Reading	193	Sunbeam F4A	1961	Burlingham	D. Lovegrove
Rotherham	37	Daimler CTC6	1950	Roe (1956)	D. E. Vickers
Rotherham	44	Daimler CTC6	1950	Roe (1956)	NTA
Rotherham	74	Sunbeam MS2	1942	E. Lancs	S. Collins & T. Bowden
South Shields	204	Karrier E4	1937	Weymann	BTS
Teesside RTB	2	Sunbeam F4	1950	Roe (1964)	WRTS
Teesside MT	T285	Sunbeam F4	1950	Roe (1964)	Teesside Municipal Museum
Teesside MT	T291	Sunbeam F4	1961	Burlingham	M. Dare
Walsall	342	Sunbeam F4	1951	Brush	BTS
Walsall	862	Sunbeam F4A	1954	Willow-brook	Black Country Museum, Dudley
Walsall	864	Sunbeam F4A	1954	Willow-brook	NTA
Walsall	872	Sunbeam F4A	1956	Willow-brook	BTS
Wolverhampton	616	Sunbeam F4	1949	Park Royal	Railway Pres. Society
Wolverhampton	654	Guy BT	1950	Park Royal	NTA
Wolverhampton	433	Sunbeam W	1946	Roe (1959)	WTG Birmingham Sci. Mus.

BPTA—Bournemouth Passenger Transport Association
BTA—Bradford Trolley-bus Association
BTS—British Trolleybus Society (formerly Reading Transport Society)
EAT Museum—East Anglian Transport Museum
EMTS—East Midlands Transport Society
LTS—Ipswich Land Transport Society

LTPS—London Trolleybus Preservation Society
NTA—National Trolleybus Association
TMS (I)—Transport Museum Society of Ireland
WRTS—West Riding Trolleybus Society
WTG—Wolverhampton Trolleybus Group

A sad postscript to the story of the trolleybus has to be recorded in the deaths a few months after the final 1972 closure of two figures who played important roles. One was Charles Owen Silvers, appointed general manager at Wolverhampton in 1915, who is regarded as producing in 1927 the first vehicle to justify the change from 'railless' to trolleybus. The other was Chaceley Humpidge, general manager at Bradford from 1951 to 1961, who did much good work for the city's fleet at a time when trolleybuses were slipping from favour. Remembered as a firm yet kindly man, he was a keen lay churchman who took holy orders after retirement from transport management at Sheffield.

BIBLIOGRAPHY

THE sources explored for this book fall into four sections. First are those relatively few commercially-published books; then books or booklets published by enthusiasts' societies, often to help finance preservation of trolleybus vehicles; third, newspapers and periodicals; and finally technical documents, papers given to various audiences, house magazines, official reports and so forth.

PUBLISHED SOURCES

Bishop, R. A. *The Electric Trolley Bus* (Sir Isaac Pitman & Sons 1931)

Brearley, H. *A History of Bradford Trolleybuses 1911–60* (Oakwood Press, Sth. Godstone 1960)

Brearley, H. *The Trolleybus 1882–1966* (Oakwood Press, Sth. Godstone 1966)

Brotchie, Alan. W. *Tramways of the Tay Valley* (Dundee Museum & Art Gallery, Dundee, 1965)

Hartshorne, D. J. *How to Install Overhead Equipment for Trolleybuses* (Tramway & Railway World Publishing, 1939)

Jowitt, Robert E. *A Silence of Trolleybuses* (Ian Allan, 1971)

Joyce, J. *Trolleybus Trails* (Ian Allan, 1963)

Kaye, David *Buses and Trolleybuses Before 1919* (Blandford Press 1972)

King, J. S. *Keighley Corporation Transport* (Advertiser Press, Huddersfield, 1964)

Mawson, J. *Bournemouth Corporation Transport* (Advertiser Press, Huddersfield, 1967)

Roberts, C. G. *Bournemouth Trams and Buses* (Oakwood Press, Sth. Godstone 1972)

Strong, L. A. G. *The Rolling Road* (Hutchinson 1956)

Symons, R. D. H. and Creswell, P. R. *British Trolleybuses* (Ian Allan, 1967)

Wilson, Geoffrey *London United Tramways* (Allen & Unwin 1971)

*   *   *

The London Trolleybus (Dryhurst Publications, 1961)

PRIVATELY PUBLISHED SOURCES

Appleby, J. B. *Bristol Trams Remembered* (Pub. by the author)

Bowen, D. G. and Callow, J. *The Cardiff Trolleybus* (National Trolleybus Association)

Brearley, H. *Railless Electric Traction in Gt. Britain* (Sheffield Omnibus Enthusiasts Society 1971)

Brearley, H. and Beach, David T. *Under Two Liveries* (West Riding Transport Society)

Brown, T. J. *The Walsall Trolleybus System* (W. Riding Transport Society)

Deans, Brian T. *Glasgow Trolleybuses* (Scottish Tramway Museum Society 1966)

Eyre, D. M., Heaps, C. W., Taylor, C. *Manchester's Trolleybuses* (Manchester Transport Museum Society 1967)

Janes, D. A. P. and Funnell, R. G. *The Trolleybuses of Portsmouth* (Reading Transport Society)

Kaye, David and Nimmo, Martin *The Trolleybuses of Brighton and Hove* (Reading Transport Society 1967)

King, J. S. *Transport of Delight. The Bradford Trolleybus 1911–72* (National Trolleybus Association 1972)

Sandford, Geoffrey *The Trolleybuses of St Helens* (Reading Transport Society)

Scotney, D. J. S. *The Maidstone Trolleybus* (National Trolleybus Association 1972)

Stainforth, J. A. L. and Brearley, H. *The Bradford Trolleybus System* (West Riding Transport Society 1972)

York, F. W. *The Trolleybuses of Birmingham* (British Trolleybus Society 1971)

*   *   *

The Huddersfield Trolleybus System (Huddersfield Trolleybus Preservation Society 1967)

London's Trolleybuses (The P.S.V. Circle and the Omnibus Society)

50 Years of Teesside Trolleybuses (National Trolleybus Association 1969)

NEWSPAPERS & PERIODICALS

Autocar
Belfast Telegraph
Bradford Weekly Telegraph for 1911
Brighton Herald
Bus and Coach
Buses Illustrated (*Buses* from 1969)
Commercial Motor
Daily Express
Daily Mercury, Leeds, for 1911

Daily Telegraph
Daily Telegraph, Bradford, for 1911
Evening Standard, London
Financial Times
Modern Transport
Telegraph and Argus, Bradford
Tramway and Railway World

OTHER SOURCES

Electrical Control Equipment for Trolleybuses (catalogue). Allen West & Co. Ltd., Brighton

Associated Equipment Co. Documents and catalogues from early 1920s

B.C.V. Gazette. House magazine of Bristol Commercial Vehicles

Brochure to Commemmorate the Termination of Trolleybus Operation. Belfast Corporation (May 1968)

Trolley-Bus & Tramway Overhead Equipment (mid 1950s). Reprinted by Brecknell, Willis & Co.

Bournemouth Trolleybuses. Bournemouth Corporation Transport (1969)

Bradford City Transport—Short History of the Undertaking to 31 March 1972

Bradford Transport Committee. Report of deputation to the Continent, submitted May 1910; and other committee records

Development of the Leyland Bus. Prepared for British Leyland Motor Corporation (2nd ed. March 1969)

Causon, G. S. and Stevens, F. G. *Substation equipment for rail and road systems*. Paper read to British Electrical Power Convention (May 1956)

Chalk, D. L. *Silent Service. The Story of Bournemouth's Trolleybuses*. Omnibus Society paper (1962)

Crosley, A. S. *Early Development of the Railless Electric Trolleybus*. Paper read to the Newcomen Society (March 1961)

Electricity Council ref. paper RP1. Also statistics 1920–72

Records and catalogues of the companies now constituting GEC (1909 onwards)

Trolleybuses in Glasgow. Glasgow Corporation Transport

Hail and Farewell. Maidstone & District. (1959)

Hatton, Ernest. Paper read to Municipal Tramways Association (November 1908)

Hawker Siddeley. Press release on electric bus (March 1972)

Honey, Philip. 'Electric Traction in Britain.' Published in *Electricity* (July 1967)

Inside Only. House magazine of Maidstone & District (February and April 1972)

London Transport. Technical Information Sheet No. 12 (May 1962)

54 Years of Public Service 1907–61 souvenir and timetable. Mexboro & Swinton Traction Co.

Ministry of Transport regulations

Ministry of Transport report into the trolley vehicle accident in Huddersfield on 4 October 1938

Railless Electric Traction Co. Ltd. Description of its demonstration system (September 1909)

Ransomes, Sims & Jefferies. Company documents 1925–39

Riley, C. F. *Nottingham's Trolleybus System.* Omnibus Society paper (1966)

Spencer, C. J. *Electric Trolley Omnibuses.* Paper read to Institution of Electrical Engineers and the Institute of Transport. (April 1933)

Tattam, C. R. Paper read to Municipal Tramways and Transport Association. (June 1933)

INDEX

811810A